THE LITTLE BOOK OF

NORTHERN IRELAND

Written by Mike Henigan

THE LITTLE BOOK OF
NORTHERN
IRELAND

This edition first published in the UK in 2010
By Green Umbrella Publishing

© Green Umbrella Publishing 2010

www.gupublishing.co.uk

Publisher Vanessa Gardner

Printed and bound in the UK

ISBN: 978-1-906635-57-2

Contents

Introduction

▼ Waves break along the shore of Ballycastle in Northern Ireland.

Northern Ireland is the smallest of the countries that make up the United Kingdom of Great Britain and Northern Ireland with 1.775 million inhabitants. Six of the nine counties of Ulster lie within its borders: Antrim, Armagh, Down, Fermanagh, Londonderry/Derry and Tyrone.

Since the start of the peace process in

1999, there has been an unprecedented growth in Northern Ireland's economy and population. The young population has seen the peace dividend produce a vibrant and successful country, although much support is needed from mainland Britain to keep the economy buoyant.

The country's history includes more than its fair share of conflict, starting with Gaelic chiefs battling among themselves, Viking and Norman invaders, Protestant settlers and planters fighting the locals and themselves, through to nationalist battles for independence and unionist attempts to resist. Its recent history of conflict is best illustrated by the fact that the Nobel Peace Prize has been awarded to four Northern Irish people, Máiread Corrigan and Betty Williams in 1976, and John Hume and David Trimble in 1998.

Northern Ireland also has more than its fair share of literary and artistic greats of worldwide fame, including Nobel Laureate Seamus Heaney, CS Lewis, Brian Friel, Kenneth Branagh, Sir John Lavery, Van Morrison and Sir James Galway, to name just a few.

This book provides an intriguing insight into Northern Ireland's history, culture and sport, government and many places of interest.

Terminology

Éire – the Irish name for Ireland and used to describe the Republic of Ireland.

Erin – commonly used in poetry and literature to describe the island of Ireland.

Ireland – the whole of the island of Ireland but also used in sport for some teams which are made up of people from both sides of the border, such as rugby and hockey.

Norn Iron – a nickname describing Northern Ireland as spoken phonetically by the local population.

The North – the generic term for Northern Ireland (where "the South" refers to the Irish Republic).

Northern Ireland – the official name for the six counties forming part of the United Kingdom of Great Britain and Northern Ireland.

Six counties – the counties forming Northern Ireland.

The Republic – the Republic of Ireland/Irish Republic.

Thirty-two counties – used to describe all the counties of the island of Ireland.

Twenty-six counties – the counties forming the Republic of Ireland.

Ulster – although often used as an alternative to the term Northern Ireland, Ulster is the province made up of nine counties on both sides of the border: Armagh, Antrim, Down, Fermanagh, Londonderry, and Tyrone in Northern Ireland, and Cavan, Donegal and Monaghan in the Republic of Ireland. The term derives from the word *Ulaidh*, the people who lived there, with *staðr,* the old Norse word for place.

History

Prehistory and Stone Age

Human occupation of Ireland came much later than other parts of Europe. After the last great Ice Age, Ireland was a frozen, barren place. When the temperatures rose and the ice retreated, land bridges to Britain and from there to Europe meant that the land was colonised by plants and animals. Around 8000BC, melting ice raised the sea levels and cut off the land bridges, preventing much flora and fauna from reaching the island. This is the real reason behind the lack of snakes in Ireland, although this was later attributed to the powers of St Patrick.

There is no evidence of human settlement at this stage. Some time after

8000BC, the earliest known humans would have arrived, probably nomadic hunters crossing the narrow straits from Scotland to Antrim (although there is also a theory that there were occasional land bridges appearing and disappearing). These hunters have left little trace other than their primitive flint instruments.

Around 4000BC, a new culture evolved through the arrival of new settlers, most likely via the Antrim route again. This was based on farming instead of hunting or simple food-

gathering and involved clearing the land
of forests, sowing seeds and harvesting
crops. Raising stock and making pottery
became a major part of Stone Age life.

It was at this stage that the
megalithic tombs built of stone started
to appear – many of which still survive;
Ballygroll Prehistoric Complex is a
prime example. Many demonstrate
some remarkable feats of logistics,
engineering and design, which suggests
that this was quite an advanced and
prosperous civilisation.

Bronze Age
and the Arrival
of the Celts

A new phase of Irish history began
around 2000BC with the Bronze Age.
It's not known if this came about through
settlers or invaders or as a result of trade.

Copper was mined and smelted
while tin was imported from Britain

▲ Navan Fort
or Emain Macha.

▶ An array of spearheads, daggers and other implements dating from the Bronze Age.

(as there are no tin mines in Ireland). Gold was also mined and used to make jewellery and other artefacts. New customs, such as the erection of henges (earthen circles) and stone circles suggest that this was a period of significant cultural development.

There is inevitably some debate about the arrival of the Celts but the most common view is that they first moved into Ireland around 500BC, coming in several waves as they fled the expansion of the Roman Empire. They brought with them the Gaelic language, the warrior culture and social structure, as well as religion involving druids and human sacrifice. They also brought the latest technology with them – iron.

By 1000AD, the Celts had established many kingdoms (*tuath*), perhaps up to 200, each ruled by a king (*rí*) who fought endlessly among themselves. There would be an overlord who had the allegiance of several kings and there was then a *rí ruirech*, who was king of a province. There is the earliest evidence of Ireland being divided into the Five Fifths – Ulster, Meath, Leinster, Munster and Connacht. Ulster's royal site was at *Emain Macha*, near Armagh. From 800AD, there appears to have been a High King of Ireland but this title was not universally accepted and carried more prestige than real power.

The Romans made a few incursions but never tried to occupy Ireland, although there is some evidence of settlement at Drumanagh, north of Dublin, and there appears to have been some trade between the Celts and the Romans. By the end of the 3rd century, when Rome's influence was starting to wane, the Irish started to establish colonies and in the 5th century the *Dál Riata* from the northeast of Ireland crossed into Argyll, Scotland, and eventually drove out or absorbed the native Picts.

It was in the 5th century that the last Roman legions left Britain and the empire disintegrated to be replaced by the barbarians. In Ireland, however, the Roman and British influence continued as Christianity took hold.

Arrival of Christianity

It is not known when the first Christians came to Ireland; however, it

▶ St Patrick, depicted with his foot on a snake in reference to his expulsion of them.

THE LITTLE BOOK OF NORTHERN IRELAND

is known that the first Irish bishop was Palladius, (sent by Pope Celestine) who established a Christian community in Leinster in 431AD.

It was St Patrick who did most to convert the Celts to Christianity. Born in 387AD to a wealthy family in northern Roman Britain (or perhaps Scotland), he was carried off by Irish marauders at the age of 16 and sold into slavery with a chieftain named Milchu near Slemish Mountain (now part of Co Antrim) who was also a druid high priest. During his six years there, he perfected his knowledge of the Gaelic language and gained a close insight into Druidism. While herding his master's flocks, he had the time to discover his Christian faith.

He eventually fled back to Britain and devoted himself to the service of God. After some years in Gaul (present-day France) training as a priest and then a bishop, he was chosen by his mentor, St Germain, to fight paganism and heresy in Britain. Some doubted his suitability, partly due to his youth and partly down to a lack of education. Despite his success in Britain, he was driven by a desire to return to Ireland, fuelled by dreams and voices of the Irish. Pope Celestine I was keen to convert

the Irish and, one year after he had sent Palladius, he entrusted St Patrick with the mission. St Patrick landed near Strangford Lough in 432 and his first conversion was that of Dichu, the local chieftain and brother of the High King of Ulster. Dichu gave him a barn at Saul and it is here that St Patrick preached his first sermon in Ireland – *Sabhal*, pronounced Saul, is the Irish for barn.

Much of St Patrick's life was documented in his own work, *Confessio* (Confession), which showed how far and wide he travelled and how difficult it was for him to convert the Irish. Apart from this, there is little to learn about his work in Ireland and there is much controversy among Irish historians about the nature of the Church in Ireland in his time. Despite 6th century historians claiming he converted the whole island – creating the "Cult of Patrick" – it seems that he stayed mainly in the northern half, based out of Armagh, while Kildare was the centre of the southern part of the Church. St Patrick died and is buried in Downpatrick, Co Down.

Through St Patrick's efforts, much of the island was converted and it was only in the 6th century that Christianity became firmly established. Many

▶ A Viking longship.

monasteries were created in bleak and remote places but there were also several endowed by local wealthy families. Old pagan habits and Celtic structures remained strong, however, relying on family hierarchies; with a reliance on the network of small kingdoms, the Irish Church developed its own distinctive character, being more loosely organised than the Roman Church and with monasteries at its centre, rather than bishoprics.

The monasteries of Ireland became centres of great learning at a time when Roman civilisation was coming to an end. Irish monks wrote masterpieces such as *The Book of Kells* and *The Book of Durrow* and were also able to preserve much of Celtic history and mythology. *The Ulster Cycle*, a series of mythological tales, would have been written in the 7th or 8th century.

During the 6th century, Irish missionaries such as St Columba (*Colm Cille*) and St Aidan were responsible for establishing monasteries on Iona and at Lindisfarne, converting the Picts of Scotland and many in northern England. St Columban, among others, spread the Christian word through Europe and St Brendan is said to have reached America.

The 7th century saw a power struggle between the two great centres of the Irish Church: Armagh and Kildare. Armagh's claim to primacy was based on its ties with St Patrick and was also supported by the Uì Neill dynasty, whose star was on the rise. By the second half of the 8th century, Armagh was able to establish its primacy unopposed.

The Viking Raiders

Ireland's isolation had protected it from the worst attacks by the Goths and the Vandals who had beset the rest of Europe but around the turn of the 8th century, the Norse Vikings began to invade the island. Small bands raided around the coast, snatching booty such as relics and jewellery and, if they couldn't find anything of value, they would take slaves. In 820, Nendrum on Strangford Lough was partially destroyed; although it was rebuilt, the Vikings raided again in 874; the monastery was sacked and burned, and abandoned forever.

The Vikings became more established, venturing further inland by following river routes. In 839, they established a fleet on Lough Neagh, making year-round raids possible, enabling the monastery in Armagh to be pillaged. Most Viking towns were effectively military bases, used for inland raids. There were some alliances between the Irish and the Vikings but in most cases there were violent skirmishes and battles.

In 848, the Irish won four battles over the Vikings and the tide seemed to be turning. In 851, the Danes arrived and began to fight the Norse, with the Irish taking advantage of the split. By 866, the dominant O'Neill clan had cleared the Vikings out of their northern settlements. The Vikings regained a hold over much of Ireland with only intermittent raids north – as demonstrated in 921, when the Norse leader Sitric sacked Armagh.

The High Kings of Ireland

Celtic traditions were firmly family-based and the main family in the north in medieval times were the O'Neills (*Uí Neills*), based mainly in *Tír Eoghan* (what is now Co Tyrone). Their prestige was helped by victories over the Vikings and, to some extent, their alliance with the church.

Although the O'Neills claimed to be the first High Kings of Ireland, this was more an aspiration than a reality. However, by the beginning of the 10th century, they were kings of Tara and held some power over much of Ireland, with the exception of Munster and Connacht.

By 1002, the king of the Southern O'Neills, Máel Sechnaill, had ceded to the increasing power and influence of Brian Ború. Over the next 12 years, Ború raided the north a number of times but despite paying homage in Armagh was never able to subdue all of the local kings. In 1014, he fought the Battle of Clontarf against the Vikings and some Irish kings allied with them.

Unfortunately Ború himself was killed and his unifying force was lost. Máel Sechnaill regained his place as Ireland's most powerful king but was never able to match the success of Brian. Upon his death in 1022, there was a fight for power among all the dynasties.

By the start of the 12th century, the four main dynasties were: the O'Briens ruling Munster; the Mac Lochlainns of the O'Neill clan ruling Tyrone and the North; the O'Connors ruling Connacht; and the Mac Murchada ruling Leinster. By 1166, it was Mac Murchada who, allied to the Mac Lochlainns in the North, held most power; however, following the assassination of King Muirchertach Mac Lochlainn in that year, Mac Murchada had to turn to King Henry II of England for military assistance against his enemies, changing the course of Irish history.

◀ Brian Ború defeated Danish invaders at the Battle of Clontarf.

▼ The Banqueting Hall area of the Hill of Tara was allegedly the seat of the High Kings.

▲ King John of England.

The Normans

the power he and other Barons held, and in 1171 arrived in Waterford with a large army to overpower the Normans and the Irish – he was then acknowledged and accepted as "Lord of Ireland".

In 1177, one of the Norman Barons, John de Courcy, invaded *Ulaid* (currently Antrim and Down), building castles at Dundrum and Carrickfergus, as well as other bases at Newry, Carlingford and Coleraine. The rest of modern-day Ulster remained under Irish control. Prince John, later King John, was responsible for overseeing much of the conquering of Irish lands and in 1199 he was given permission by the Pope to declare himself King of Ireland. De Courcy defeated King John in 1204 but was eventually captured and sent to the Tower of London before dying in exile in France in 1219.

By 1300, the Normans controlled most of Ireland – with the exception of Ulster – however their hold then began to weaken. The struggle between the Scots and the English led to Edward Bruce, brother of Robert the Bruce, attempting to become High King of Ireland. Edward landed near Larne and moved southwards, defeating the Normans on the way. He was crowned

Mac Murchada was reinstated thanks to the Normans' superior weapons and tactical skills. He rewarded them with lands throughout Leinster. One of his key allies was Richard de Clare, Earl of Pembroke – also known as Strongbow – who eventually ruled Leinster himself. However, Henry II was concerned about

in 1316 but was defeated and killed two years later.

The Irish realised that they could regain territory on their own and the combined effects of intermarriage with the Irish, taking on Irish customs – becoming "more Irish than the Irish", as it was later described – and the Black Death in 1348-49 also helped undermine Norman rule. Richard II tried to regain control in the 1390s but was unable to do so. By the 15th century, Norman control was restricted to an area around Dublin, known as "the Pale" (leading to today's expression "beyond the Pale", meaning uncivilised or out of control).

▲ Richard II knighting the four Kings of Ireland.

THE LITTLE BOOK OF NORTHERN IRELAND

The Tudors

The Tudors had a major influence in Ireland. In 1485, after the War of the Roses, Henry VII was proclaimed King of England and reasserted English rule in Ireland with some success, getting oaths of allegiance from many Irish chiefs, except for the O'Neills. Henry VIII was recognised as King of Ireland (not just "Lord") and was able to persuade the then head of the O'Neills to take the title Earl of Tyrone, although his successor then repudiated the title. Despite his break with the Roman Church in 1531, he only had limited success in promoting the Reformation in Ireland and the country remained primarily Catholic. Queen Mary (despite being a Catholic) and Queen Elizabeth I (who re-established the Protestant Church in England) both continued the Tudor tradition of trying to "plant" English settlers around Ireland, as well as introducing an element of English administration and the division of the provinces into shires.

There were various Irish revolts at the time, all put down with great ferocity by Elizabeth's deputies. Sorley

Boy MacDonnell (*Somhairle Buí*) and his family were sworn enemies of the O'Neills and also fought the English, defeating them at Carrickfergus in 1552. He was captured by Shane O'Neill in 1565 but then defeated him and had him killed two years later when O'Neill was guest at a feast. In 1575, Sorley Boy sent his wife and children to Rathlin Island for safety but, on the orders of Walter Devereux, 1st Earl of Essex, they and the 600 inhabitants were massacred as Sorley Boy watched from Tor Head on the mainland.

▲ The first coat of arms for O'Neill is believed by some to simply be the Red Hand of O'Neill on a shield.

◄ Rathlin Island from Tor Head, scene of the massacre.

Nine Years War and the Flight of the Earls

The most serious of the rebellions started in 1594, led by Hugh O'Neill, a Court favourite of the Queen who had taken the title Earl of Tyrone in 1585. By 1595 he had thrown down the gauntlet to the Queen and assumed the title "The O'Neill", setting himself out as the chief of Gaelic Ulster – she ultimately declared him a traitor.

Hugh Maguire of Fermanagh began the rebellion by supporting his fugitive cousin, Red Hugh O'Donnell, and expelling the English administration. Hugh O'Neill was asked by Elizabeth to help put down the rebellion, although O'Neill's men fought on both sides at this stage. O'Neill joined forces with Maguire soon after the Battle of the Ford of the Biscuit – a name arising out of the sight of English rations floating down the River Arney near Enniskillen.

The rebellion lasted until 1602 when O'Neill was driven out of Ulster by the burning of Dungannon by

Lord Mountjoy. O'Neill had expected help from the Spanish but their troops arrived in the southern port of Kinsale, too far away to be of much use. O'Neill finally surrendered in 1603, shortly after the death of Elizabeth.

O'Neill was, however, left with most of his possessions and became friends with his victor, Mountjoy, until the latter's death in 1606. O'Neill's English and Irish enemies started to move against him and he and his allies decided to flee to the continent in 1607 – an event which became known as "the Flight of the Earls". O'Neill's strongholds were finally dismantled, leaving the whole of Ireland subjugated to the English.

▲ Hugh O'Neill making a formal submission to the English after the suppression of his Irish rebellion.

◄ Hugh O'Neill led the resistance during the Nine Years War.

Plantation

Soldier and statesman, Oliver Cromwell.

St Oliver Plunkett, the Irish Catholic Prelate.

The English response to the rebellion was to "plant" Ulster with English and Scottish Protestants. The Flight of the Earls had left much of Ulster without their landowners so the best land was given away to those loyal to King James II. Land was given to former soldiers, compliant locals, lowland Scots, the English and the (Protestant) Church. Derry was given to the City of London and its various livery companies, and these were tasked with developing the city commercially. It was renamed Londonderry – a name which is still highly political.

Learning from the failures in other parts of Ireland, where settlers were regularly attacked and driven out, towns were set up across Ulster to provide protection to the settlers. For the most part, the settlers were Scottish Presbyterians (although still covered by the broad term "Protestants"). Their religion, farming methods and puritan lifestyle set them apart from the rest of Ireland. They were not concerned to convert the Catholics but equally were not able to drive them out completely.

With Charles I's accession to the throne and the ensuing English Civil War, Catholic landowners in Ireland, both Irish and English, saw an opportunity to seize power – the idea of a deeply Protestant Parliament had filled them with fear. In 1641, there was a rising in Ulster led by Sir Phelim O'Neill that saw many Protestants massacred and that year is much commemorated in Ulster Protestant history. There were massacres of the Catholics as well but these have not been commemorated to the same extent.

The subsequent years saw struggles between the different factions, old and new Irish, old and new English and Scots settlers. The most decisive action came in August 1649 when Oliver Cromwell's army of 20,000 landed in Dublin. By the time he returned to England in May 1650, Ireland was firmly under English control. Outside Ulster, Irish landowners had been expelled to the colonies in the West Indies or had their lands confiscated and handed to those loyal to Cromwell.

The restoration of Charles II to the throne did not change anything, for fear of a Protestant backlash. Religious and political intolerance was relatively rare, although there was a constant fear in England and Ulster of popish plots. In 1679, St Oliver Plunkett, the Archbishop of Armagh and Primate of All Ireland, a Catholic, was tried in England and convicted of high treason, then executed on 1 July 1681. He was canonised in 1975.

Upon the death of Charles II, his brother James II – a Catholic – acceded to the throne. With this threat to Protestant rule, and upon the birth of a Catholic son to James in 1688, the English Parliament asked William of Orange and his wife Mary (James' Protestant daughter) to take the throne. James fled to France but sought to use Ireland as a base for his comeback and raised his Catholic Jacobite army. Ulster, however, had sided with William and Mary.

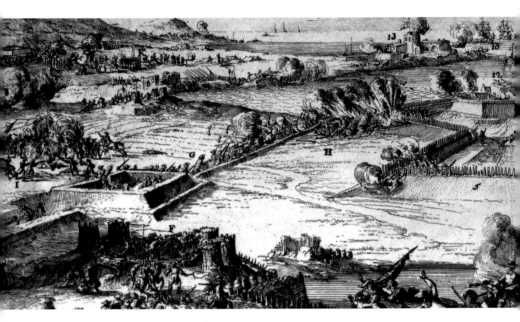

Siege of Derry

▲ The Siege of Derry, 1689.

In April 1689, the Jacobite army marched on various strongholds in Ulster – including the garrisons at Derry and Enniskillen – hoping to control the whole of Ireland. In Derry, the loyalist organisation, the Apprentice Boys, who had been sent over from the City of London, were able to shut the gates to prevent the Jacobite forces from entering. A boom was placed across the River Foyle and the city was cut off and besieged for 105 days. The siege was finally lifted in July when a Williamite ship, the *Mountjoy*, managed to breach the boom. James fled Derry. The Apprentice Boys of Derry – with more than 10,000 members – still celebrate the closing of the gates and the lifting of the siege.

The following month, William's army landed at Carrickfergus and took the town. Ireland then became a battleground for the wider European struggle for and against Protestantism. Louis XVI of France sent troops to aid James, while William was helped by troops from Holland, Denmark and other anti-French allies from the Grand Alliance. The two armies met at the Battle of the Boyne in Co Meath on 1 July 1690 (now celebrated on 12 July). William was victorious and James fled to France. Although James' army continued to fight, they surrendered in October 1691 and the war ended with the Treaty of Limerick. Most of the Jacobite soldiers were allowed to flee to France and became known as "the wild geese".

Penal Laws

▶ The growing of flax enabled the Belfast linen industry to flourish.

After the Treaty of Limerick, a series of Penal Laws were passed that were designed to rid Ireland of Catholicism. Catholics were excluded from all political power, ownership of land was severely restricted, they could not own a horse worth more than £5, could not hold any profession other than that of doctor – these harsh measures forced many Catholic landowners to convert to the Anglican Church. In 1728, Catholics were completely disenfranchised. Although the Laws were widely used in the early days, they were generally not so strictly enforced – greed being the main driver behind their enforcement, rather than any religious bigotry.

Most of the Catholic population in Ireland was utterly impoverished at this stage and was largely unaffected by these Laws. However, in Ulster, many Catholics worked on the lands for the Protestant owners and then in the linen trade that started to grow around Belfast. A Catholic middle class eventually grew, although their loyalty had to be seen to be to the Crown.

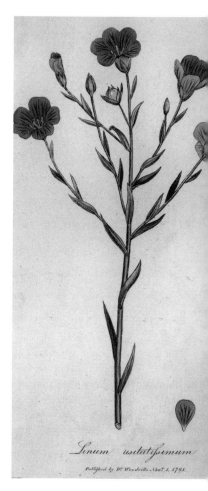

Linum usitatissimum

Published by D.ʳ Woodville Nov.ʳ 1. 1791.

Presbyterian Exodus

Many Presbyterians (also known as "dissenters") were also discriminated against in terms of the professions and political office – although they were allowed to practice their religion, they were only permitted to officially be part of public life in 1780. They were allowed to hold land but these were usually smallholdings and the best land was kept for Anglicans. Many were unhappy with their situation and the exodus from Ulster to North America began in 1717 – the first year when an emigrant ship was officially recorded leaving from Derry, with records showing a total of 5,000 emigrants that year.

An estimated 250,000 Ulstermen emigrated between 1720 and 1775.

THEOBALD WOLFE TONE.

Political Upheaval and Revolution

Despite the discrimination, most of the 18th century was relatively peaceful. Driven by the hard life on the land and attracted by the prospect of work in the linen factories and other industries springing up, Catholics started to gravitate towards the major towns and cities, living mostly in slum conditions and with occasional outbreaks of sectarian violence. At the same time, a large Protestant middle class grew, engaging freely in commerce and politics.

The late 18th century should be seen against the background of two major political changes: American Independence in 1777 and the French Revolution in 1789.

Many Protestant landowners and businessmen had resented the power of the Westminster Parliament and there was concern and alarm about the relaxation of the Penal Laws through various relief acts. They agitated for an Irish Parliament, which was recognised

in 1782 as a separate and independent institution under the Crown.

The French Revolution in 1789 added to Protestant insecurities. By 1791, the French had offered to help any group wanting to overthrow their King, leading to war with Britain, Spain, Germany and Austria. The war meant that Prime Minister William Pitt needed stability in Ireland, as well as a steady flow of cannon fodder for the war.

That year was also notable for the founding of the Society of United Irishmen in Belfast. Driven by the ideals of the French Revolution, they sought to have a united Ireland of all faiths with greater economic and political independence from Britain. They gained support from the more liberal business and commercial classes in Belfast and were then able to set up a branch in Dublin. However, their pro-French

▲ The Irish House of Commons.

◀ Irish nationalist Wolfe Tone.

▲ Marching season in Northern Ireland.

tried on several occasions to start a rebellion but had failed. In June 1798 an uprising started in Wexford, in the southeast of Ireland, and the Antrim branch decided they had to join in or be wiped out. The Antrim uprising lasted only a few days and the French support arrived in the west of Ireland in August, too late to help.

The Orange Order

During the worst times of the Penal Laws, various groups of rebels had formed secret societies to protest against ill-treatment and the collection of tithes (a form of taxation). In the north, the organisation was known as the "Defenders" and the Protestant equivalent was the "Peep O'Day Boys". Things reached a climax at the so-called Battle of the Diamond on 21 September 1795 when the Peep O'Day Boys killed a number of the Defenders. That evening, the Peep O'Day Boys met again and established the first Orange Order Lodge. They vowed to stand and fight for their church and

ideals were viewed as treasonable and the British set out to quash the Society, both through their intelligence network of informers and more importantly through brute force. The Orange Order, founded in 1795, was against them and militia of yeomen were formed to root out the radicals, using terror and destruction to force their submission.

The Society, led by Wolfe Tone, had

"support, maintain and defend the Protestant succession". By the end of the year, there were more than 90 lodges, all commemorating the Battle of the Boyne.

Over the years, the Orange Order has been seen as a defender of the Protestant faith and of ties to England and Britain. The Order has been at its strongest whenever Irish nationalism has threatened the Protestant majority, particularly during the struggles over Home Rule and Partition. During the Troubles, there were allegations of strong links between the Order and loyalist paramilitary groups.

The order is organised into private "lodges", with every Orangeman belonging to his own lodge, of which there are several around the world in former British colonies. The next level up is the district lodge, then the county lodge, with the Grand Orange Lodge of Ireland at the top of the organisation. Orange Halls are prevalent in the north and are often at the centre of the Protestant community (and as such have been targets for sectarian violence and vandalism).

Orange parades have been the focal point of much controversy. The main date for parades is 12 July, commemorating

the Protestant victory at the Battle of the Boyne. Orangemen see it as their right to parade and celebrate their culture, while nationalists often see the parades as a symbol of bigotry and sectarianism. Drumcree in Portadown was the focus of many standoffs and violence in 1995 and subsequent years, although since the peace process has taken hold, most parades now take place without serious incident.

▼ The regalia of the Orangemen for No 9 District, West Belfast.

Act of Union

William Pitt decided that military force was not the only solution. A union of the British and Irish Parliaments, making Ireland a part of the United Kingdom, was the only way forward. Using a great deal of bribery and granting of honours, the Act of Union became law on 1 January 1801 and the United Kingdom of Great Britain and Ireland came into being.

Following the Union, laws passed in Westminster became even more repressive. Although expected after the Union, Catholic emancipation was not granted. There was a minor uprising by the United Irishmen, led by Robert Emmet, in Dublin in 1803. In the north, magistrates and juries were made up of men who belonged to the Orange Order and laws were enforced with injustice and cruelty.

The liberal Presbyterians of the north took some time to overcome the traumas of their support of the United Irishmen and in the 1820s politics were dominated by two men, Henry Cooke and Henry Montgomery. Cooke was able to reconcile the Presbyterians and

Arrah! be aisey honey till we'll get emancipa-tion — then we'll let ye loose on the Heretics

O'Connel for ever

Suit the Action to the Word

The devil a mothers son of us but would stick a pike into the guts of the first Man in the Kingdom who refuses it !

Down with the Heretics !

Bl—dy murder to the rogue who dares to oppose Catholic Emancipation !

Hurra! boys, Long life to the King! hide your weapons under rags, ye Spalpeens till I'll tell ye's to use them — Hurra! boys — down wid the the heretics !!!

To CLARE   To LONDON

No Faith to be kept with Heretics

Catholic Rent roll

O'Connel for ever

Persecution

Oath of Allegiance

Emancipation

the Anglicans in Ulster and persuade a majority of them to accept the Union. Montgomery was a radical and in favour of emancipation. Cooke prevailed and in 1840 helped to establish the General Assembly of the Presbyterian Church, a Unionist stronghold to this day.

In 1823, in the south of Ireland, Daniel O'Connell formed the Catholic Association that had two central aims: to reform the last of the Penal Laws and to

▲ A cartoon depicting Daniel O'Connell leading an angry mob toward London to demand Catholic emancipation.

▶ Daniel O'Connell addressing a meeting.

improve conditions for tenant farmers. By 1828, O'Connell felt bold enough to stand for Parliament in Co Clare, although as a Catholic, he was unable to take his seat. Through his agitations (he was in favour of peaceful protest), the laws were changed to allow both Catholics and Dissenters to become MPs and hold Crown office, although this was counterbalanced by legislation

that disenfranchised many Catholic voters by abolishing the voting rights of small farmers.

O'Connell then sought to repeal the Union itself, forming the Repeal Association in 1840. Through his "monster meetings" in the south, he was able to build up strong support for repeal. His one visit to Belfast in 1841 was not a success. Although he had many Catholic supporters, he did not directly confront his adversary Cooke and his visit lasted only four days. His efforts may well have eventually succeeded but Ireland's situation was transformed by the devastation of the Great Famine of 1845–50.

◀ Starving people searching for potatoes in a stubble field during the Great Famine.

The Great Famine

Ireland's population had doubled to more than 8 million between 1800 and 1840, possibly reaching 9 million by 1845. In most of Ireland, the peasant masses subsisted on tiny farmholdings and were reliant on a single crop, the potato. The landlords cared little for what happened on the land as long as

▲ A priest
visiting a
destitute family.

they received their rent. The potato
blight first appeared in 1845 and
completely destroyed the potato crop in
1846. The effect in most of Ireland was
devastating, compounded by epidemics
of typhus, fever and cholera that swept
the island. Migration to North America

became the only salvation for many.

On the whole, Ulster was spared
the worst of the effects of the blight.
The system of landholding gave tenants
better security, farms were better
managed and not so reliant on the one
crop. Industrialisation had taken hold

and most of the province was wealthier than the rest of the country.

Migration from the wealthier parts of Ulster was not as common as the rest of the country, although those that did leave headed mainly for Canada. However, Fermanagh (along with Monaghan and Cavan) suffered terribly: from 1841 to 1851, more than 26% of the population was lost either to famine and disease or to migration.

Industrialisation

After hard times in the early 19th century, in much of the north, industries such as linen, rope and glass manufacture, tobacco and iron foundries began to thrive. Shipbuilding also came to the fore: by 1851, the famous shipbuilding firm Harland & Wolff had completed its first ship. Belfast and the

◀ Workers leaving the Harland & Wolff shipyard, 1911.

THE LITTLE BOOK OF NORTHERN IRELAND

Lagan Valley were the centres of this industrialisation but Londonderry also benefited. The transport network was improved: in 1837, access to Belfast port was improved by the dredging of its main channel; during the 1840s, a railway network was created, linking Belfast with towns such as Ballymena, Lurgan, Portadown and Armagh.

Belfast's population grew substantially throughout the second half of the 19th century: in 1841 it was 75,000, by 1851 it was up to 98,000 and by 1901 it had reached 387,000. This partly reflected economic growth but was also down to the effects of the famine. Many of those who sought refuge in the towns were Catholic. At the turn of the 19th century, only 10% of Belfast's population was Catholic but by 1861, this had risen to more than 34% before falling to 24% by the beginning of the 20th century.

The period also saw an increase in religious division – both Protestant and Catholic churches became more authoritarian and conservative and the differences became more marked, with religious identity becoming part of each group's identity, Catholics with nationalism and Protestants with unionism.

The First Push for Home Rule

The famine had demonstrated to many that Ireland should not be ruled from Westminster but should have its own parliament, known as "Home Rule". There was also an increase in Irish nationalism: a brief but unsuccessful revolt in 1848 and the growth of the Fenian movement with support from the Irish in America and a further rising in 1867.

The Liberal Prime Minister William Gladstone, came to power in 1868 and saw it as his mission to "pacify Ireland". He introduced measures such as the disestablishment of the Church of Ireland and the right for tenants of church land to buy out their property. In Parliament, Irish MPs committed to Home Rule, led by Charles Stewart Parnell, began to hold up proceedings with filibusters. Gladstone introduced a Home Rule Bill but this split his own party and in the 1886 election he was defeated by Lord Salisbury's Conservatives who strongly opposed Home Rule.

◀ The Royal Irish Constabulary protecting a government reporter at a meeting of Charles Stewart Parnell's supporters.

▲ Police charging demonstrators during the Belfast riots of 1886.

Gladstone returned to power in 1892 and the following year introduced a new Home Rule Bill with a slower devolution of power. Although passed in the Commons, the House of Lords defeated the Bill, which at the time meant it could not be passed. Gladstone resigned a year later and the Liberal government was defeated in 1895.

The Unionist Response

In Ulster, Home Rule was viewed by Unionists as a threat to Protestant supremacy and their support from across the Irish Sea. There were regular sectarian

THE LITTLE BOOK OF NORTHERN IRELAND

clashes between working class Protestants and Catholics, particularly in Belfast. The local police force was financed out of local taxation and was seen as partisan. It was abolished in 1864, replaced by a centralised force controlled out of Dublin.

Political marches had been banned in 1850, although some continued to take place. In 1867, William Johnston defied the ban by leading an Orange march from Newtownards to Bangor; he became a local hero, was elected an independent MP and was successful in repealing the laws against processions in 1872.

In 1886, Randolph Churchill visited Belfast. He was strongly opposed to Home Rule: he felt that it could lead to the break-up of the British Empire, there was an obligation to support those loyal to British rule and, most importantly, he saw the possibility for returning Conservatives to power. He was ready to play the Orange card: "Ulster at the proper moment will resort to its supreme arbitrament of force. Ulster will fight, and Ulster will be right."

That year saw a summer of rioting in Belfast with 50 people killed and nearly 400 injured. "Roaring" Rev Hugh

Hanna was among those who inflamed the passions of both working class and middle class Protestants from the pulpit.

The second Home Rule Bill in 1893 stirred Protestant protests even more. William Johnston passed a motion at Union Hall in Belfast that Home Rule should be resisted passively. His fellow Unionists responded with intermittent rioting and agitation. On 4 April,

▲ William Gladstone introducing the Home Rule Bill in the House of Commons.

▲ William Gladstone introduces the Home Rule Bill.

▶ Pope Pius X who brought out the law regulating marriages between Catholics and Protestants.

Rule with kindness" by redressing economic grievances and giving tenants credits to buy land they had worked from their landlords.

However, the Unionists were not idle and felt the need to be more organised. The 1890 bi-centenary of the Battle of the Boyne had been much celebrated and had provided a strong focus for unionist resistance. In March 1905 they formed an Ulster Unionist Council made up of about 200 members, led by Col James McCalmont, MP for East Antrim. This council was to play a significant role in resisting the Home Rule Bill.

Ulster Resistance

100,000 loyalists were joined by Arthur Balfour, Chief Secretary for Ireland and a future British Prime Minister, before a rally at Linen Hall. By September, the Bill had been defeated in the House of Lords, and with the Conservatives and Unionists in power from 1895 the threat of Home Rule had receded. The new government sought to quieten nationalist tendencies and "killing Home

In 1906 the Liberals returned to power with a landslide victory. They did not need the Irish nationalists to vote with them and were able to avoid a divisive third attempt at introducing Home Rule. The situation changed with the general election of 1910, when the Liberals again became dependent on the support of the Irish party, led by

John Redmond. The Irish MPs insisted on the House of Lords losing its right of veto as a price for their support – it would only be able to delay legislation. The third Home Rule Bill looked like it would be passed in the summer of 1914, however by this stage resistance was fierce, enflamed more and more by the feeling that Catholic rule from Dublin would be disastrous or worse.

One example used arose out of Pope Pius X's *Ne Temere* decree in 1908. Until then, mixed marriages between Catholics and Protestants were relatively common in Ulster, especially in the west of the province. The decree required explicit approval of any mixed marriage by a Catholic priest and at least two witnesses. This meant that priests could insist that the children of all mixed marriages be brought up as Catholics and that any non-Catholic party to the marriage be required to be re-educated and convert. This reinforced the unionist idea of "Home Rule or Rome rule".

The unionists, led by Sir Edward Carson and Sir James Craig, began to make preparations for forceful resistance. Drilling and military manoeuvres took place, with recruiting drives organised through Orange and Apprentice Boys'

lodges. Ulster Day in September 1912 saw 218,000 Ulstermen pledging to use all possible means to resist Home Rule – the "Ulster Covenant" – and the Ulster Volunteer Force (UVF) was formed shortly afterwards.

With the passing of the Home Rule Bill looking ever more likely, 1914 saw Ulster coming close to civil war. In March, 58 of 70 British Army officers based at the Curragh near Dublin threatened to resign their commission if required to enforce Home Rule in Ulster and the War Office looked like it could lose control of its army in Ireland. In April, 25,000 German rifles and 3 million bullets were unloaded at Larne, with the police doing nothing to stop it. Plans were made for the evacuation of civilians and an Ulster currency had been designed. Serious consideration was being given to the nine counties of Ulster being allowed to opt out of Home Rule. Carson had hoped that by asking for all nine counties to be able to opt out, it would make Home Rule unpalatable to the nationalists.

On 4 August 1914, Germany invaded Belgium and Britain declared war. The Ulster problem was put on hold.

The Great War

Ulster Protestants wanted to demonstrate their loyalty to the Crown and joined the army in their thousands. The Ulster Division (commonly known as Carson's army) was formed and became a part of unionist legend when 5,500 men were killed in a single day at the Battle of the Somme. Catholics also joined the army, partly encouraged by Redmond's belief that a display of loyalty would make Home Rule more likely when the war was over, but also out of economic necessity – army pay was much better than the benefits on offer at home. These National Volunteers were not offered their own division but were dispersed throughout the army. In all, 200,000 Irishmen joined the army and more

◄ Members of the Protestant Orange Order marching through Belfast in 1914.

▼ British troops climbing from their trench on the first day of 'The Big Push' on the Somme during the First World War.

▲ Sir Roger Casement being escorted to the gallows.

than 60,000 were killed, with Protestants and Catholics suffering equally.

In the south of Ireland, the Irish Republican Brotherhood (IRB) saw "England's difficulty as Ireland's opportunity" and the Easter Rising took place on Easter Monday 24 April 1916, with a proclamation of an Irish Republic. The rising was confined to Dublin and was short-lived but the British reaction in executing many of its leaders altered the mood of the country outside Ulster.

One of those executed after the Easter Rising was Sir Roger Casement. He was from a Protestant family in Antrim who had gone to the Congo as a British diplomat and had been knighted as a result of his work in exposing the brutalities of the Belgian regime there. After becoming involved in the Gaelic League in Ulster, he then joined the Irish Volunteers. He was sent to Germany to seek help but was rebuffed and returned to call off the Rising; however he was arrested and never got to pass on the message. Following the Rising and the humiliation of having his homosexuality revealed through his diaries, he was hanged as a traitor on 3 August 1916.

The War of Independence and Partition

Although the question of Home Rule was officially on hold, Prime Minister David Lloyd George continued dialogue with Carson and Redmond. However, more ardent nationalists, led by Eamon De Valera and the *Sinn Féin* movement (literally "ourselves alone"), were able to make the most of the revulsion felt by many over the British reaction to the Easter Rising. By the time of the first post-war general election in 1918, Sinn Féin was able to win 73 of 105 Irish seats, to six for Redmond's Irish party. Unionists won 26 seats.

Sinn Féin refused to go to Westminster and set up their own parliament, Dáil Éireann, in Dublin. In contrast to this constitutional approach, the Irish Republican Army (IRA, formally the Irish Volunteers or IRB) then fought a vicious war of independence, helped by contributions from the USA. The British response was heavy-handed and

the Royal Irish Constabulary (RIC) was supplemented by the notorious "Black and Tans" – recruited from among unemployed demobilised British troops, their name coming from their mix of dark police uniforms supplemented by khaki army uniforms

▲ A petrol can, revolver and pepper pot symbolising Sinn Féin's objections to the Anglo-Irish Treaty and the partition of Ireland.

▲ The Irish peace conference.

– and the Auxiliaries (or "Auxies"), an elite, commando-style force.

In Ulster, unionists remained implacably opposed to any form of nationalist rule. 1920 became a key year in the history of the north. There was strong support for Sinn Féin in Londonderry (or "Derry" as nationalists call it) and sectarian riots broke out between April and August, with more than 50 people being killed. The army threatened extreme measures against both sides and nationalist support fell away. Specialist constabularies – later becoming known as the Royal Ulster

Constabulary (RUC) – were set up in November 1920, made up wholly of UVF members. Most notorious of these were the B-specials who were virulently anti-Catholic. There were occasional riots in towns around the north but the most serious attacks on Catholic property were in Belfast. Catholics were heavily outnumbered and badly armed, so were not able to retaliate to any great extent.

In December 1920, Lloyd George's government passed the Government of Ireland Act, making partition a reality with separate devolved parliaments in

Dublin and Belfast. Northern Ireland comprised the four counties with strong unionist majorities, Antrim, Armagh, Down and Londonderry, and two additional counties with strong unionist representation, Tyrone and Fermanagh, to make the new province a stronger social and economic entity. The other Ulster counties of Donegal, Cavan and Monaghan had declining Protestant populations and were left out. In the election of May 1921, Unionists won 40 of the 52 seats and Sir James Craig became the first Prime Minister of Northern Ireland.

As the war of independence became increasingly bitter and expensive, Lloyd George realised he had to sue for peace and asked De Valera and Craig to attend a peace conference and a truce came into effect on 11 July 1921. On 6 December, the Irish delegation accepted the Treaty and the Irish Free State officially came into being in 1922. Northern Ireland was allowed to opt out and retain the status it had since 1920, with a Boundary Commission determining the exact line of the border. The UK was renamed the United Kingdom of Great Britain and Northern Ireland.

Post-Partition

Many nationalists in the south felt that the six counties could not survive on their own and would eventually agree to unification. They could not have been more wrong, as demonstrated by Craig's determination not to give an inch of the country during the Boundary

▼ Stormont, home to the Northern Ireland parliament.

▲ A patrol car on the streets of Belfast after the 1935 riots.

Commission's review of 1924.

Northern Ireland was effectively left to run its own affairs through the parliament at Stormont. Although there was a substantial Catholic minority of about one-third, they were not in a position to rebel, and in fact they felt abandoned by the Free State. Between 1920 and 1922, 232 Catholics and 157 Protestants were killed and security

was ruthlessly enforced, with the RUC having draconian powers of search, arrest and detention, used mainly against the minority. Unionists dominated local and central government, as well as the RUC, and Catholic representation at senior level was minimal at best. By repressing the nationalist Catholic population, the unionist Protestants were able to protect their interests and at the same time keep

THE LITTLE BOOK OF NORTHERN IRELAND

the demographic balance by forcing Catholics to emigrate, counterbalancing their higher birth rate.

Even in predominantly Catholic areas, rules were changed or bent to ensure unionist dominance. Gerrymandering (the distortion and manipulation of political boundaries to suit one party) was rife. In Derry City, Lloyd George had guaranteed a system of proportional representation (PR) – a Catholic mayor was elected in 1920 but by 1922, PR had been abolished and a Catholic mayor was not elected again until 1968. Although excluded politically and to some extent economically, Catholics were by and large able to live peacefully; there was occasional rioting – after an Orange parade in Belfast in 1935, there were nine days of riots and nine deaths, with more than 500 Catholics driven from their homes.

The standard of living remained higher in Northern Ireland than in the Free State, helped by its industrial strength and its linen and shipbuilding industries in particular. It also did not have the burden of a bitter civil war to deal with. However, the Great Depression of the 1930s affected its main industries and overall unemployment remained high until the outbreak of the Second World War. The economic situation brought about a spate of rioting, often involving both sides fighting together against the police.

The war brought some prosperity through the thousands of American troops stationed in the North and new industries such as aircraft manufacturing. The downside was that Belfast and Derry were exposed to the German's Blitz, something which the administration had not expected – in April 1941, both cities were targeted with 900 people killed and 10,000 made homeless.

After the war, the economy revived, with foreign investment in the north, although this was mostly in the east of the country, where the unionist population was dominant. However, all sides in the north benefited from the British welfare state and the free health and education services on offer – from the earliest days, Sir James Craig (later Lord Craigavon) had insisted that whatever was provided in Britain would also be provided in the north. Although there was still much poverty among Catholics, with slums in Derry

▲ Young men throwing stones in the Falls Road of Belfast.

▶ Armed British soldiers patrolling the streets of Belfast.

and Belfast, a Catholic middle class had grown up and there was little to upset established order. There was an IRA campaign – Operation Harvest – that ran from 1956 to 1962, involving guerrilla raids from bases south of the border on various targets in the north. Internment without trial was imposed and in 1957 Sinn Féin was banned north of the border but the campaign eventually petered out through lack of support from northern Catholics.

The Start of the Troubles

The established order was shaken up in the mid-1960s, after years of stagnation. A low-key meeting took place between Terence O'Neill, the Northern Irish Prime Minister, and Seán Lemass, the Irish Taoiseach (prime minister), ostensibly to discuss closer economicties

When Jack Lynch became Taoiseach in 1966, he continued the dialogue. The grassroots Protestant reaction was predictably loud and clear, led by the fierce oratory of Rev Ian Paisley. They objected in particular to articles in the Republic's constitution which claimed jurisdiction over the whole of Ireland and which placed the Catholic Church in a special position. Meanwhile, militant Protestants were becoming involved

with a resurgent UVF.

On the other side, there was an increased awareness among the newly educated Catholic Northern Irish of the inequalities and injustices being perpetrated against them. This led to the foundation of the Northern Ireland Civil Rights Association (NICRA) in January 1967. The allocation of council houses was one great source of irritation, as well as the decision to set

▼ British soldiers sorting through a weapons cache in Belfast.

up Northern Ireland's second university near (Protestant) Coleraine, rather than (Catholic) Derry, the more obvious choice to many.

In late 1968, the NICRA and other student groups had organised protest marches that were violently broken by the RUC and B-specials, actions that were captured by television cameras and shown around the world. By July 1969, sectarian violence was widespread in Derry and Belfast and the Catholic minority was in danger of being overwhelmed. Derry saw a three-day battle between the Catholic population of Bogside and the RUC. The Northern Ireland government was persuaded to ask Westminster for help and on 16 August, British troops were sent in and welcomed as peacemakers. UK Prime Minister Harold Wilson also ordered Stormont to reorganise and disarm the RUC, disband the B-specials and improve community relations.

The Catholic population initially welcomed the troops but did not entirely trust them and turned to the Republic and to the USA for help in the form of money, arms and ammunition. At this point, the Provisional IRA – named after the Provisional government of 1916 which had usurped the traditional ("Official IRA") leadership, began to gain influence among the Catholic population and used civil unrest to their advantage.

The Troubles

The Provisional IRA ("Provos") was able to recruit among disaffected Catholics in the slums of Belfast and Derry but recruitment was made easier by the approach of the authorities to the trouble, in particular the violent and aggressive searches for arms on the Catholic Falls Road in Belfast and internment without trial. Internment had worked well in counteracting the IRA campaign in the mid-1960s but it now meant that many innocent men were detained, particularly from the Catholic community, and levels of resentment were very high.

One anti-internment march led to one of the north's most infamous dates: "Bloody Sunday" on 30 January 1972. After the march, rioting broke out and the army believed it was under attack from the IRA. As a result, troops from the Parachute Regiment opened fire on the rioters, killing 14, with none of those killed found to have been armed. The subsequent inquiry was viewed as a cover-up by nationalists, there was fresh rioting and the IRA stepped up its campaign.

The government wanted to re-arm the RUC and re-establish the B-specials but the UK government decided to act. It took control of the RUC and appointed a Secretary of State; the Stormont government resigned en masse but British PM Edward Heath responded by introducing direct rule from London through the Northern Ireland Office. Internment was then abolished.

The Protestant community had already felt seriously threatened and this new turn of events saw the escalation of loyalist rioting, civil unrest and attacks on nationalists. By the end of 1972, 496 lives had been lost on both sides, the worst annual toll of the Troubles.

▼ Coffins of 13 civilians shot dead by British troops on Bloody Sunday being lined up for a funeral.

▲ Talks taking place at Sunningdale to establish a Council of Ireland.

allowing Protestants and Catholics to share power. Assembly elections were held in June 1973, with a majority of unionists in favour of power-sharing. However, the Sunningdale Agreement of December 1973 raised the prospect of the Republic having a say in Northern Irish affairs. Anti-agreement unionists were outraged and were able to use the British general election of 1974 to derail the process. They won 11 of the 12 Westminster seats and, when the assembly confirmed its support for Sunningdale, a general strike was called by the Ulster Workers' Council on 17 May. The assembly resigned on 28 May and direct rule was reintroduced, lasting for a further 25 years.

Atrocities

During the course of the Troubles, the effects were felt in other parts of the British Isles, with IRA/INLA (Irish National Liberation Army) bombings and assassinations in London, Manchester, Birmingham, Guildford and Warrington. Loyalists bombed Dublin and Monaghan in 1974, killing 33, but their actions were mostly confined to the north.

Sunningdale

In 1973 and 1974, the British government sought to re-establish a new government of Northern Ireland,

The Troubles saw many atrocities, murders and deaths. Some of the most notorious ones are listed below.

McGurk's Bar, Belfast, 1971 – the UVF's first atrocity, killing 15 pub goers. "Bloody Friday",

Belfast, 1972 – nine killed by a series of IRA bombs.

"Bloody Monday", Claudy, 1972 – a succession of IRA bombs killed nine civilians.

Miami Showband Massacre, Banbridge, 1975 – three band members shot dead by the UVF after a bomb being planted in their bus went off prematurely. Two bombers died.

Kings Mills, 1976 – 10 Protestant construction workers taken off a minibus and killed by IRA gunmen. The Catholic driver of the minibus was spared.

La Mon House Hotel, Belfast, 1978 – 12 people killed in a hotel restaurant.

Warrenpoint, 1979 – 18 soldiers killed by two bombings, with one civilian killed by crossfire in a subsequent firefight.

Dropping Well, Ballykelly, 1982 – 11 soldiers and six civilians killed by an INLA bomb at a disco.

Darkley Gospel Hall, 1983 – three worshippers gunned down at a Sunday evening service.

Newry Police Station, 1985 – nine police personnel killed in an IRA mortar attack.

Remembrance Day, Enniskillen, 1987 – 11 killed by an IRA bomb.

Downpatrick, 1990 – four UDR (Ulster Defence Regiment) soldiers killed by an IRA bomb.

Teebane Crossroad, Co Tyrone, 1992 – eight killed by an IRA bomb.

Ormeau Road, Belfast, 1992 – five civilians shot by Ulster Freedom Fighters (UFF) in a bookmakers.

Shankill Road, Belfast, 1993 – nine killed by the IRA in a fish shop; one bomber died.

▼ Crowds in Belfast marching in support of the prisoners on hunger strike.

Greysteel, 1993 – eight killed by gunfire from members of the UFF in revenge for the Shankill Road bombing.

The Heights Bar, Loughinisland, 1994 – the UVF's last atrocity, killing six Catholics as they watched a World Cup football match.

The worst of all the bombings in the North came in **Omagh** on **15**

August 1998 when 29 people and two unborn children were murdered, and hundreds injured, by a car bomb planted by dissident republicans, the Real IRA.

It should not be forgotten that many suffered at the hands of their own paramilitaries, with punishment beatings, kneecappings and other violence being used to bring the communities into line.

The Hunger Strikes

The hunger strikes in 1981 led to the deaths of 10 IRA and INLA prisoners and were the culmination of protests at the Maze Prison (also known as Long Kesh or the H-blocks, so-called because of their shape). Initially, these took the form of prisoners refusing to wear prison uniform, then escalating to a "dirty protest", with prisoners refusing to slop out and smearing their cells with excrement. The hunger strikes began on 1 March, started by Bobby Sands. They were given greater prominence by his election as MP for Fermanagh and South Tyrone on 9 April. The British government refused to accede to the strikers' demands and Sands died on 5 May. The final hunger striker to die was Michael Devine on 20 August. Eventually, many of the strikers were persuaded to stop by their families and the strike ended on 3 October. In total, 13 others had joined the hunger strikes at various stages.

The hunger strikes had demonstrated

▲ Sinn Féin supporters during a Bobby Sands commemoration march.

to Sinn Féin that they could wield
political power in the North – the
strategy of the armalite and the ballot
box – and they began to win seats in
local elections and Westminster elections,
most notably when Gerry Adams
defeated Gerry Fitt, a centre-ground
nationalist, in West Belfast in June 1983.
This raised the prospect of Sinn Féin
becoming the leading nationalist party,
overtaking the moderate SDLP, which
was a worrying prospect for both the
UK and Irish governments.

The Peace Process

The start of the beginning of the peace
process could be said to have been
the Anglo-Irish Agreement, signed
by British Prime Minister Margaret
Thatcher and Irish Taoiseach Garret
FitzGerald in November 1985. This
confirmed that Northern Ireland
would remain independent as long as

that was the will of the majority in the North but the Republic gained a say in the running of the country through an Intergovernmental Conference to discuss security and political issues. Although unionists protested, nationalists said it was not enough and paramilitary violence continued for another decade; the seeds had been sown.

unionists had a right to object, leading to a key constitutional change in the Republic. By this stage, US President Bill Clinton was bringing his influence to bear, particularly on the nationalists.

In 1994, the IRA announced a "complete cessation of military activities", with the UVF and UDA

▼ Gerry Adams leaving No 10 Downing Street after his meeting with Tony Blair.

Talks and Ceasefires

Talks took place over the following years between the main loyalist and nationalist parties, although Sinn Féin and the loyalist PUP and UDP were excluded until a ceasefire was agreed by their respective paramilitary counterparts. In 1988, a broadcasting ban began against Sinn Féin and other paramilitary organisations.

December 1993 saw the Downing Street Declaration by Prime Minister John Major and Taoiseach Albert Reynolds; this accepted the principle of self-determination for all the people of Ireland, including the possibility of a united Ireland. Dublin accepted that

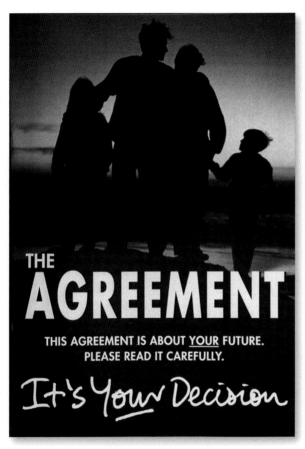

THE **AGREEMENT**

THIS AGREEMENT IS ABOUT <u>YOUR</u> FUTURE.
PLEASE READ IT CAREFULLY.

It's <u>Your</u> Decision

IRA had ended its ceasefire with the Docklands bombing in London and Sinn Féin was excluded from talks until 1997 when a new ceasefire was ordered. In October 1997, Gerry Adams met Prime Minister Tony Blair for the first time.

The Good Friday Agreement

On Friday 10 April 1998, the Belfast Agreement (also known as the "Good Friday Agreement") was signed, providing for devolved government in Northern Ireland on a stable and inclusive basis. It also provided for the early release of terrorist prisoners, the decommissioning of paramilitary arsenals and far-reaching reforms of criminal justice and policing arrangements. The Agreement was endorsed by referendum on 22 May 1998. The fundamental aspects to the process that are vital to its continuing success are dealt with below.

On 25 June 1999, the first elections to the Northern Ireland Assembly

following shortly after. The broadcasting ban was lifted. By February 1995, the

took place, with the UUP and SDLP voted as the largest parties and the DUP, who were against the Agreement, coming third. However, the power-sharing was to have a chequered history over the next few years. There were disagreements over decommissioning and the unionists were very mistrustful of Sinn Féin and the IRA. While other elements of the peace process made progress, devolution was suspended on 14 October 2002 when there was a police raid on Sinn Féin's offices during an investigation into republican intelligence gathering. Although the Assembly continued to sit as a transitional assembly, it had no executive powers. It wasn't until 26 March 2007 that devolved government returned to Northern Ireland.

▲ Democratic Unionist Ian Paisley and Sinn Féin's Gerry Adams sit around the table to discuss devolution.

◀ The Stormont Agreement.

Geography and Historic Sites

For such a small area, Northern Ireland has a wide variety of scenic countryside and major cities (such as Belfast, Londonderry/Derry, Armagh, Newry and Lisburn) as well as many historic sites and monuments. There is a World Heritage site, prehistoric settlements, Norman castles, beautiful coastline, mountains of magic and mystery and a wide variety of churches to grab the visitor's attention as highlighted in this chapter.

Outstanding Natural Beauty

Perhaps the most famous spot of all in Northern Ireland is the **Giant's Causeway** (*Clochán na bhFómharach*), a UNESCO World Heritage site since 1986. According to legend, the Causeway was formed by a giant, Finn MacCool (*Finn mac Cumhaill*), who tore large pieces of rock from the cliffs to make a causeway to Scotland to fight an adversary, Benadonner. When "discovered" by the Bishop of Derry in 1692, some thought that it must have been created by men with tools.

In reality, it is a natural phenomenon, formed more than 60 million years ago out of more than 40,000 massive black basalt columns rising out of the sea. Its mainly hexagonal pattern is formed as a result of the crystallisation of lava combined with accelerated cooling.

The Giant's Causeway is part of the spectacular 12-mile **Causeway Coast** which extends along the north Antrim coast to the Carrick-a-Rede rope bridge. Much of the area is owned by the National Trust and is designated an Area of Outstanding Natural Beauty (AONB). Following several years of political controversy, the National Trust is now expected to build a new £18.5 million visitors' centre by the end of 2011.

The **Carrick-a-Rede** rope bridge provides an exhilarating experience, with visitors walking a 20-metre wide chasm with a 23-metre drop to the sea below. The bridge was originally used by fishermen to check their salmon nets and had a single rope hand rail, replaced by a two-hand rail bridge and now with a caged bridge installed in 2000 as a result of health and safety fears. Before the latest bridge, many visitors had to travel back to the mainland by boat, unable to face going back across the bridge.

◄ The basalt columns of the Giant's Causeway.

The Carrick-a-Rede bridge that links Carrick Island to the mainland.

Here are some other points of interest along this part of the Antrim coast:

• **Antrim Glens**, an Area of Outstanding Natural Beauty, which covers some 50 square kilometres with many changes in natural landscape, from glacial valleys to sandy beaches, wooded glens and picturesque villages. There are nine Glens – Glenarm, Glencloy, Glenariff, Glenballyeamon, Glencorp, Glenaan, Glendun, Glenshesk and Glentaisie – and the area is well known for its richness of culture and friendliness.

• **The Chimneys**, or Lacada Point, was the site of the 1588 wreck of the Spanish Armada galleon *Girona*. Heading for shelter in Catholic Scotland, she foundered on the rocks as a result of bad weather and more than 1,300 lives were lost, with fewer than 10 survivors. Local folklore tells of many victims being buried in St Cuthbert's graveyard next to Dunluce Castle.

• **Rathlin Island** (also known as Raghery) lies at the northernmost point of Ireland, only 3 miles off the coast of Antrim and 16 miles from the Mull of Kintyre in Scotland. Shaped in an "L", it is 10 kilometres (6 miles) long and 1.6 kilometres (1 mile) wide. The island is steeped in history, with many ancient cairns and tombstones, church and castle sites. The island also has a large colony of seabirds. Rathlin's most famous tale concerns Robert the Bruce who took refuge here in 1306, after being driven from Scotland by Edward I of England. While on the island, it is said that he watched a spider persevering again and again to bridge a gap with its web, eventually succeeding. He took heart from its endeavours and raised fresh forces before returning to Scotland to fight for his kingdom which he regained in 1314.

The **Mountains of Mourne** – made famous by Percy French's song, where an emigrant to London yearns for the mountains "that sweep down to the sea" – form part of the Mourne AONB, covering just over 57,000 hectares. With more than 150,000 visitors annually, it is also one of the most popular tourist spots in the North. Of the Mourne's 12 peaks, Slieve Donard (850 metres, 2,788 feet) is the highest point in Northern Ireland, below which there is a rich variety of habitats, including heather, moor, bog and upland pastures, through freshwater and woodland to lowland heath. Although offered some protection by its status as an AONB, there are plans to designate the Mournes as Northern Ireland's first National Park, providing additional protection

to wildlife and habitat and boosting tourism in the region. The idea is not without controversy as many feel that the regulations involved would place too many restrictions on farmers and traditional industries like sand, gravel and granite production, as well as drive up house prices for locals.

Some of the finest beaches and dune systems in Ireland can be found at **Binevenagh** – designated as an AONB in 2006 – an area which includes Magilligan Strand, a fine, sandy beach that is 8 kilometres (almost 5 miles)

▼ The southern part of Rathlin Island.

 Looking
towards the
Mountains of
Mourne.

long. The spectacular railway journey
from Coleraine to Londonderry follows
the coast through Binevenagh and
features in Michael Palin's *Great Railway
Journeys of the World*.

Lower Lough Erne is the larger
of the two Loughs – 42 kilometres/26
miles and 19 kilometres/12 miles
respectively – which form part of the
proposed "Erne Lakeland" AONB. It
is part of a magnificent waterway with
154 islands and myriad coves and inlets.
Its shoreline is rich in monuments and
ecclesiastical sites.

Just outside Belfast lies the **Lagan
Valley Regional Park**, with a rich
heritage of monuments, archaeological
sites and historic buildings, including

relics of the linen industry. The
Park covers 4,000 acres including a
17.6-kilometre (10.9-mile) stretch of
the River Lagan from Stranmillis, Belfast
to the Union Locks in Lisburn.

The coastal area between Strangford
Lough and the Mournes is known as
the **Lecale Coast**, with secluded sandy
beaches, delightful coves and dramatic
headlands. The coastline is also famed
for its colonies of seals.

The **Ring of Gullion** is a rare
natural geological formation known
as a ring dyke, dominated by the steep
slopes of Slieve Gullion – a mountain
with mysterious, magical qualities
arising from its rich association with
Irish legends and myths. The area is well

THE LITTLE BOOK OF NORTHERN IRELAND

known for its cultural identity, expressed in poetry, music, folk history and art.

Lying in the heart of Northern Ireland, the **Sperrin** is a largely mountainous area with dramatic scenery, forests and lakes. The area is rich in historic and archaeological heritage and folklore. Designated an AONB in 2008, it covers 118,217 hectares (290,000 acres).

Strangford Lough is an almost landlocked inlet of the sea covering some 150 square kilometres (93 square miles). At its northernmost tip, it is only 6 kilometres (3.7 miles) from Belfast. Thirty-two kilometres (20 miles) away, the southern entrance to the Lough is the Narrows, a deep, fast-flowing channel about 8 kilometres long; at its narrowest point, it is only 500 metres wide. With its large variety of habitats, the Lough has an exceptionally rich and varied marine life, with more than 2,000 animal and plant species identified.

The largest lake in the British Isles, **Lough Neagh** measures over 300 square kilometres – it contains enough water to fill 7 million swimming pools, 800 billion gallons. Of the six counties, only Fermanagh does not have shoreline on the Lough. According to legend, it was created by the giant Finn MacCool who

▲ Lough Erne.

dug out the ground to throw at a Scottish giant who was fleeing Ulster over the Giant's Causeway; the piece of land he threw ended up as the Isle of Man. With the wide variety and huge number of birds that pass through its shores, the Lough attracts birdwatchers from all over the world. Angling and fishing are also major attractions. Outside tourism and leisure, the Lough's major industries are eel fisheries and sand dredging for the construction industry.

Castles, Walls and Historic Buildings

▲ Belfast City Hall.

The **Walls of Derry** were completed in 1619 as defences for settlers from England and Scotland, and are one of the finest examples of walled cities in Europe. The Walls vary in width between 3.65 metres and 10.66 metres (12-35 feet). The entire building cost was met by the Irish Society, a group of London businessmen responsible for the Plantation of Derry. It was their duty to build and maintain the Walls to help control the local Irish rebels. Despite sieges in 1641, 1649 and the Great Siege

▲ The ruins of
Dunluce Castle.

of 1689, the Walls were never breached. The 24 surviving cannons were restored in 2005 and form the largest collection in Europe – Roaring Meg, built in 1642 and used in the siege of 1689, is the most famous of all and sits on its traditional location on the Double Bastion.

Built in response to Queen Victoria's grant of a charter to the City, **Belfast City Hall** was completed in 1906 and dominates the heart of the city. Sir Brumwell Thomas' design covers an area of about an acre and is built out of Portland Stone. The main rooms are the Council Chamber, the Great Hall, the Reception Room and the East Staircase.

Dunluce Castle sits dramatically on the edge of a headland with cliffs falling away to the sea. It was built in the 13th century, with substantial additions

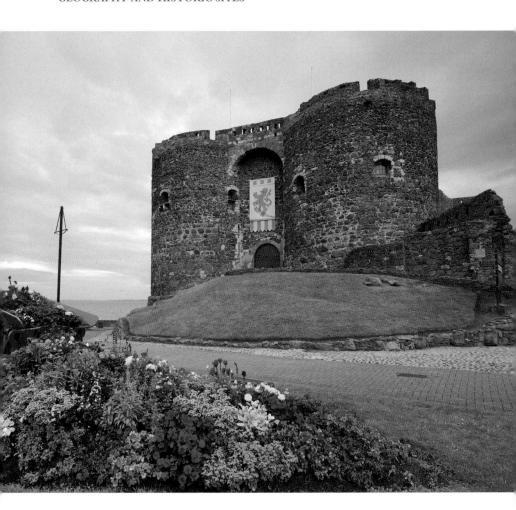

in the early 17th century, by the first Earl of Antrim. Its demise began in 1648 after one of the great kitchens fell into the sea; it was abandoned in 1690 as the family had sided with James II and became impoverished after he was defeated at the Battle of the Boyne in 1690. The castle was given to the Northern Ireland Government by the Earl of Antrim in 1928 to be preserved as a national monument.

Hillsborough Castle is an 18th century mansion (not a castle!) built in the 1770s by Wills Hill, 1st Marquis of Downshire. It is now the official residence of the Secretary of State for Northern Ireland and has been witness to many of the major events forming part of the current peace process, including the signing of the Anglo-Irish Agreement in 1985 by the UK Prime Minister Margaret Thatcher and Irish Taoiseach Garret FitzGerald. One of its claims to fame is that the gardens contain Europe's largest rhododendron bush.

Carrickfergus Castle sits menacingly on the shore of Belfast Lough and dominates the approach to the city of Belfast. It was built by the Normans in the 12th century, has played a vital military role throughout

its history and was garrisoned continuously for 750 years before being decommissioned in 1928. At various stages it has been besieged by the Scots, Irish, English and French and saw action as an air raid shelter during the Second World War. The castle marks the point where King William III landed in Ireland on 14 June 1690 before going on to defeat King James II at the Battle of the Boyne.

Tully Castle, overlooking Lough Erne, had a brief and tragic history, lasting 26 years. Completed in 1615, it was pillaged, burned and abandoned for good in 1641 after the Christmas Day massacre by rebels of 16 men and 69 women.

The original **Benburb Castle** also had a brief history. Completed in 1614 on the site of an earlier castle, it was captured by rebels with the familiar story of a massacre in 1641 and then dismantled in 1646. A 19th century house was built on part of the site and it now forms part of the Benburb Valley Park, Castle and Heritage Centre.

Enniskillen Castle is situated by the River Erne in Co Fermanagh guarding one of the key passes into Ulster. It was built almost 600 years ago and its history can be traced from its beginnings as a

◀ Carrickfergus Castle.

▶ Belfast Castle.

Maguire castle until its use as a barracks in the 1700s and 1800s. Throughout the 16th century the junior branch of the Gaelic Maguires ruled Fermanagh from Enniskillen Castle, their stronghold being captured and retaken many times by the O'Donnells, O'Neills and the English. There are now two museums housed within the castle: Fermanagh County Museum and the Royal Inniskilling Fusiliers Regimental Museum.

Killyleagh Castle was described over a century ago as "… pricking castellated ears above the smoke of its own village and towering like some chateau of the Loire above the tides of Strangford Lough." It could be said that nothing much has changed. The village of Killyleagh grew up around a fortified tower, built in the 12th century by the Norman knight John de Courcy, conqueror of Ulster. Today, it is the oldest inhabited castle in Ireland. The castle has self-catering apartments within the castle's towers, providing visitors with a unique holiday experience.

Belfast Castle dominates the city skyline, sitting 120 metres (400 feet) high on the slopes of Cave Hill. The first castle was built by the Normans in the late 12th century, with a new stone and timber version being completed in 1611. This burnt down in 1708 and it wasn't until 1870 that the current building was completed. The castle and surrounding estate was given to the City of Belfast in 1934. It is now a popular venue for wedding receptions and other private functions.

Built by John de Courcy at the beginning of the 13th century, shortly after the Anglo-Norman invasion of East Ulster, **Dundrum Castle** is one of the finest Norman castles in Northern Ireland, with views to the sea and the Mourne Mountains. Its location guards the land routes from Drogheda via Greencastle to Downpatrick.

Greencastle Royal Castle was built in the mid-13th century by the Anglo-Normans and defended the southern approaches by land and sea to the Earldom of Ulster, commanding the ferry link with Carlingford. It was besieged and captured in 1316 and continued in use as a garrison until the early 17th century, despite being wrecked on many occasions.

Harry Avery's Castle near Newtownstewart was built around 1320 by a local Irish chieftain and is unusual in that they rarely built stone castles at

he time. Captured by the English in 609 it was then used as a quarry for building material.

Jordan's Castle in Ardglass was built in the 15th century and is the largest of a group of tower-houses that protected what was then an important town and port. It was named after Simon Jordan who withstood a long siege in 1601.

Bellaghy Bawn has its origins as a 17th century fortified house and bawn (the defensive wall around an Irish tower house), although it now has a mix of buildings. Opened to the public in 1996, the site includes a variety of exhibitions on local history, natural history and poetry by local Nobel Laureate, Seamus Heaney.

Ancient Sites

▼ The megalithic tomb at the centre of the Giant's Ring.

Mountsandel Fort, Coleraine, is the name of a Mesolithic site that contains the oldest known settlement in Ireland. Flint tools found at the site indicate that Stone Age hunters camped here from about 7000BC to fish salmon in the natural weir. The earthen fort on the site was used from the early medieval period until the 17th century.

The **Ballygroll Prehistoric Complex** in Co Londonderry is a remarkable concentration of prehistoric monuments ranging in date from 4000 to 1000BC. The earliest is a court tomb dating to the Neolithic period and there are two wedge tombs, cairns stone circles and field walls, all reported to be the remains of a Stone Age settlement.

The **Giant's Ring** near Belfast is an earthwork circle, over 200 metres (220 yards) in diameter, built in about 2700BC during the Neolithic period, and said to be one of the finest henge monuments in Britain and Ireland. In the middle of a bank of gravel and boulders is a tomb made up of five upright stones and a large capstone.

Discovered in the 1940s, the **Beaghmore Stone Circles** near Cookstown is a complex of early Bronze Age megalithic features, stone circles and cairns. *Beaghmore* translates as the "moor of the birches", reflecting the origins of the area as woodland before being cleared by Neolithic farmers. Hearths and deposits of flint tools discovered at the site have been carbon dated to 2900-2600BC.

Navan Fort is one of Northern Ireland's most important ancient monuments and was the royal seat of the Kings of Ulster and the province's ancient capital. The Navan Centre reopened in July 2008 and offers visitors

unique insight into local legends and
folklore. The fort itself comprises a large,
240-metre (787-foot) circular earthwork
enclosing two monuments on the
hilltop, a ring barrow (Iron Age burial

site) and a large mound, believed to have
been constructed in 95BC. The site is
also identified as the legendary *Emain
Macha*, the sacred place of a military
dynasty, the Red Branch knights.

Monasteries and Churches

▼ Devenish Island Monastery.

The **Antrim Round Tower** and **Bullaun Stone** are reminders of Antrim's ancient monastic settlement which was destroyed in 1018 and finally burned in 1147. Known locally as The Steeple, it was built in the 10th century as a bell-tower for protection from raiders.

One century after the death of St Patrick, St Molaise founded **Devenish** **Island Monastery** in the 6th century. It was raided by the Vikings in 837 and burned in 1157 but flourished in the Middle Ages as the site of the parish church and St Mary's Augustinian Priory. The 30-metre (98-foot) round tower was built in the 12th century and can still be climbed today.

Nendrum Monastery was founded on Mahee Island in Strangford Lough in the 5th century by St Machaoi. A small Benedictine Cell was founded in the late 12th century and it was a parish church in 1306 before being abandoned in favour of Tullynakill Church.

Inch Abbey is a Cistercian abbey founded by John de Courcy in 1180 beside the River Quoile, probably on the site of an earlier church or monastery. It was distinctively an Anglo-Norman foundation and in 1380 Irishmen were debarred from entering the community. The abbey was burned in 1404 and monastic life ended in 1542. The ruins were handed to the state in 1910.

Grey Abbey was founded by John de Courcy's wife, Affreca, in 1193 and is the first truly gothic structure in Ireland. It was dissolved in 1541 but refurbished

or use as a parish church in the 17th and 18th centuries.

Lying in the National Trust village of Cushendun in Antrim, **Cushendun Old Church** is a simple, rectangular red sandstone building built in 1840 with room for about 80 worshippers. The church (but not the graveyard) was deconsecrated in 2003 due to a dwindling congregation but the local community wanted to save the building and develop its future as a community arts centre. It won the Northern Ireland regional heat for BBC2's *Restoration Village*, helping its funding drive considerably.

The City of Armagh is home to two **St Patrick's Cathedrals,** one Church of Ireland and one Roman Catholic. St Patrick founded his main church on Sally Hill in 445AD and there has been a Christian church on the site ever since. Partially destroyed by Viking invaders in the late 9th and early 10th centuries, a lightning strike in 995 left the church in ruins for 130 years. It has since undergone many restorations and repairs, the last being to many of the windows in 2005. The remains of the Irish High King, Brian Ború, were interred at the cathedral. The Roman

▲ The Antrim Round Tower.

Catholic cathedral, started in 1840 and dedicated in August 1873, lies on Sandy Hill across the valley from its counterpart. The site also has close links to St Patrick – when he first took possession of Sally Hill, a deer and her fawn are said to have jumped out of the bushes; St Patrick would not allow them to be killed and carried the fawn to Sally Hill, closely followed by its mother. The cathedral was finally consecrated in July 1904.

Other Landmarks

▲ Scrabo Tower.

One of Northern Ireland's best known landmarks, **Scrabo Tower** near Newtownards, provides fine views over Strangford Lough and the whole of North Down; on a clear day, there are distant views of the Isle of Man and the Scottish coast. Erected in 1857, the 41-metre (125-foot) tower was built by local people as a monument to the 3rd Marquess of Londonderry as a result of his attempts to alleviate suffering during the potato famine.

Precariously perched on the edge of

in the grain-growing area of east Co Down but all are now in ruins with the exception of **Ballycopeland Windmill**. Built around the turn of the 19th century, it fell into disrepair before being restored to full working order in 1978.

◄ Mussenden Temple.

▼ Ballycopeland Windmill.

an Atlantic cliff, **Mussenden Temple** is a small but striking circular building which served as a library. It was built in 1785 by the Earl Bishop of Derry in the grounds of Downhill House (now a ruin) and named after his cousin, Mrs Frideswide Mussenden. Owned by the National Trust, the cliffs have been stabilised to avoid it being reclaimed by the sea.

Windmills were once very common

Government, Economy and Transport

Government

On Friday 10 April 1998, the Belfast Agreement was signed, providing for devolved government in Northern Ireland on a stable and inclusive basis. It also provided for the early release of terrorist prisoners, the decommissioning of paramilitary arsenals and far-reaching reforms of criminal justice and policing arrangements. The Agreement was endorsed by referendum on 22 May 1998 and the first Assembly elections took place on 25 June.

There are three strands to government in Northern Ireland:

- The Assembly, Executive and Civic Forum, dealing with internal matters.
- The North-South Ministerial Council and Implementation Bodies, dealing with relationships between Northern Ireland and the Republic of Ireland.
- The British-Irish Council and the British-Irish Intergovernmental Conference, dealing with bi-lateral cooperation between the UK and Ireland.

The UK Secretary of State for Northern Ireland, through the Northern Ireland Office, remains responsible for all constitutional and security issues, particularly law and order, policing and criminal justice. The Westminster government retains the right to suspend the Assembly and the other institutions of government of Northern Ireland, which it has used during the peace process.

▶ Loyalist and Republican symbols on a gable end in Belfast.

Northern Ireland Assembly

The Northern Ireland Assembly is based at Stormont in Belfast and has 108 members, known as MLAs. There are 18 constituencies, each one with six MLAs who are elected on a single transferable vote system. Most of the work of the Assembly is done through its 17 departmental and standing committees, together with ad hoc committees set up for a specific purpose.

The Executive

The Northern Ireland Executive comprises 12 ministers representing 10 departments plus the Office of the First Minister and Deputy First Minister. It meets to discuss and agree on issues that cut across the responsibilities of two or more ministers. Ministers are appointed according to party strength using a detailed mechanism known as the d'Hondt system.

Policing and Criminal Justice

The policing of Northern Ireland has changed considerably since the Agreement. Following the establishment of an Independent Commission under Chris Patten, a number of changes have taken place:

A Policing Board was established with nationalist participation and extensive powers to hold the police to account. Sinn Féin joined the Board in May 2007.

The Police Service of Northern Ireland (PSNI) was set up to replace the old RUC. A new badge and uniform were agreed and there is a 50:50 split for new recruitment of Catholics and non-Catholics.

District Policing Partnerships were set up across the country to give local people a stake in policing.

A Police Ombudsman service was put in place to deal with complaints about police conduct.

The criminal justice system has also been overhauled, providing more transparency and accountability.

A number of new, independent institutions were set up, such as the Northern Ireland Judicial Appointments Commission (NIJAC), Criminal Justice Inspection Northern Ireland (CJINI) and the Public Prosecution Service (PPS).

Human Rights and Equality

The Agreement established two other bodies: the Human Rights Commission which aims "to protect and promote the human rights of everyone in Northern Ireland in law, policy and practice" as well as advising on the scope for a Bill of Rights specifically for Northern Ireland, and the Equality Commission set up with a mission "to advance equality, promote quality of opportunity, encourage good relations and challenge discrimination through promotion, advice and enforcement".

Various groups have also been set up to deal with the legacy of the Troubles, victim support and the reconciliation process, although a "Truth Commission" along the lines of the one in South Africa has been ruled out.

Economy

Northern Ireland's economy was traditionally based around shipbuilding, textiles and rope manufacture; however, in recent years it has developed around technology and services. The economy has grown substantially as a result of the peace dividend and has regularly been among the fastest growing regions of the UK. Production has fallen as a result of the global recession but not to the same extent as the rest of the UK. The state contributes an enormous amount to the economy and there are concerns that previous levels of subvention are unsustainable.

▲ Microsoft which has a facility in Queen's Island, Belfast.

◄ An armed police officer in riot gear.

The government offers financial incentives for overseas companies to set up business and also provides research and development funding.

Foreign companies to have set up include Microsoft, Oracle, Accenture, Bombardier, Seagate, Fujitsu, Caterpillar and Polaris Software. There is a highly-

educated and skilled workforce with close ties to universities. Some funding has come from the European Union but in 2008 the EU set up a task force to encourage more applications for regional grants.

Northern Ireland has an advanced telecoms infrastructure and has become the first region in Europe to have 100% access to broadband and will be the first to migrate to BT's 21st Century Network (21CN), a new global high-speed telecoms infrastructure.

Icons of Engineering and Science

Northern Ireland has many who have made contributions to the advancement of science and technology down the years. Here are some of the most well known:

Harry Ferguson, an engineer who played a key role in the development of the modern agricultural tractor. His name lives on in Massey Ferguson tractors.

William Reid Clanny is best known for inventing the Clanny safety lamp for miners, a precursor to the Davy lamp.

Professor Frank Pantridge was responsible for the portable cardiac defibrillator in 1963, realising that many deaths through cardiac arrest were avoidable if treated early.

Sir James Martin was an engineer who invented the airplane ejector seat and Martin-Baker is a leading manufacturer of the seats.

The first British vertical take-off and landing (VTOL) aircraft, the Short SC1, was built in 1957 at **Shorts** in Belfast.

William Pirrie (Viscount Pirrie) grew up in Co Down and became chairman of shipbuilders Harland & Wolff, being at the forefront of development in marine engineering.

Thomas Andrews was head of design at Harland & Wolff, overseeing the construction of *RMS Titanic*, built at their Belfast shipyard. He died aboard the ship on its maiden voyage, last seen staring into space in the first class smoking room, with his lifebelt discarded.

John Stewart Bell was a quantum physicist and philosopher who investigated quantum theory in great depth and was responsible for Bells

◀ Harry Ferguson with a toy tractor.

THE LITTLE BOOK OF NORTHERN IRELAND

Theorem, "the most profound discovery of science".

Dame Jocelyn Bell Burnell, an astrophysicist, discovered the first radio pulsars as a PhD student with two colleagues, both of whom received a Nobel Prize for the discovery; her exclusion from the award was much criticised.

Other renowned physicists include **Sir David Bates**, a specialist in molecular and atmospheric physics, and **Sir Joseph Larmor**, specialist in electricity and thermodynamics.

Transport

Northern Ireland's road network is extensive, with more than 24,800 kilometres (15,000 miles) of public roads. The first motorway was built in 1962 and there are now 148 kilometres (92 miles) in total. The roads carry more than 89% of freight traffic.

The railway network in Northern Ireland covers about 342 kilometres (210 miles). The main links are from Belfast to Larne, Derry and Bangor, together with the main Belfast-Dublin line via Portadown and Newry. There are also links from Antrim to Lisburn.

The main airports in the country are at Belfast International (also known as Aldergrove), 5.2 million passengers in 2008, George Best Belfast City Airport, 2.56 million passengers, and City of Derry Airport, 439,000. Just over 50,000 tonnes of freight pass through the airports. The country's main seaports handled 24.485 million tonnes in 2006. The main ports are Belfast (with about 60% of traffic), Larne (17%) and Derry (9%). Over half a million tourists passed through Northern Ireland's ports in 2006.

◄ Thomas Andrews died aboard the ship he helped design.

▼ George Best's father and sister at the unveiling of the George Best Belfast City Airport sign.

Culture

▶ Van Morrison
in concert,
September 2009.

▶▶ Clodagh
Rogers who
represented
the UK in the
Eurovision Song
Contest.

Ulster's culture comes from two separate communities, loyalist/Protestant and nationalist/Irish, each of which has a different set of values and attitudes and its own history. However, this doesn't mean that there is a divide – the two cultures have come together in particular since the peace process and there is a great deal of overlap and intermingling.

Northern Ireland has more than its fair share of cultural icons across sport, film and TV, music, art and literature, as well as the sciences.

Music

There is evidence of a long pre-Celtic tradition, but it was the harp that became Ireland's dominant instrument during the Celtic and Norman era, with master harpers being much in demand. Traditional Irish music as we now know it – with the fiddle, flutes and whistles, the *bodhrán* and the accordion – probably only evolved in the late 17th and early 18th centuries. Dancing with jigs and reels then became one of the most popular Irish pastimes, particularly as it was very cheap. The *ceilidh* (pronounced "kaylee") is a well-known term for an Irish (or Scottish) musical party. Of course, Ireland's great storytelling tradition is also upheld through its ballads and *sean-nós*. Another Irish

instrument of note is the *uilleann* pipes, the Irish bagpipes. In modern times, there has been a successful blending of traditional and modern music and Northern Ireland has produced several musical icons such as: **Clodagh Rogers**; **Dana**; **Feargal Sharkey**; **Gary Moore**; **Van Morrison**; **Angela Feeney**; **Sir Hamilton Harty**; and **Sir James Galway**.

Film, Stage and Television

Northern Ireland has produced a number of big screen stars over the years, as well as many faces and names which would be well-known to international and British viewers: **Amanda Burton**; **Ciarán Hinds**; **James Nesbitt**; **Kenneth Branagh**; **Sam Neill**; and **Liam Neeson**.

In the world of television, some of the familiar names and faces on screen are: **Eamonn Holmes**; **Patrick Kielty**; **Gloria Hunniford** and her late daughter **Caron Keating**; **Gordon Burns**; **Jackie Fullerton**; and **Zoë Salmon**.

Literature and Art

Even before the monasteries began to write down some of the Celtic folklore, Ireland had a great tradition of storytelling. The north has produced some great writers, philosophers and poets.

The Ulster Cycle is one of the four cycles of Irish mythology – the others being *The Fenian Cycle*, *The Mythological Cycle* and *The Cycle of Kings*. It is a group of 80 heroic stories set in Ulster and Connacht around the beginning of the Christian era, dealing with the *Ulaid*, the people who gave Ulster its name. It deals with the lives of Conchobar mac Nessa, the great warrior Cúchulainn, the son of Lugh, and of their friends and enemies, as well as their lovers. The stories centre round the royal court at Emain Macha, near Armagh.

A Presbyterian from Belfast, **Robert Macadam** (1808-95), played a vital role in the preservation of Irish literature. He was responsible for preserving many Irish manuscripts from the north and west of Ireland at a time when the

◄ Seamus Heaney, one of the greatest living poets.

◄◄ James Nesbitt, star of television and the big screen.

British government was looking to stamp out many traces of Irish culture. He collected, transcribed and translated many of the works, often interviewing Irish speakers for their stories.

The most famous of modern poets from Northern Ireland is **Seamus Heaney**, who won the Nobel Prize in Literature in 1995. He has commented on the fact that his mixed background

of the cattle-herding Gaelic past and the Ulster of the industrial revolution led to a "quarrel with himself", out of which his poetry comes. He has been very active in promoting artistic and educational causes, both at home and abroad. His wife, **Marie Devlin Heaney** is an author in her own right.

Heaney was one of a group of poets who came to be recognised as a "Northern School" within Irish writing. The others were his contemporaries **Michael Longley** and **Derek Mahon**, followed later by **Ciaran Carson**, **Medbh McGuckian** and **Paul Muldoon**. Heaney, Longley and Mahon were prominent members of the "Belfast Group", writing workshops driven by the energetic lecturer in English, Philip Hobsbaum. Heaney admitted that this workshop had considerably helped develop their work.

Prior to the emergence of the Northern School, **Samuel Ferguson** and **John Hewitt** had been the most significant Irish poets from the north, together with **Robert Greacen**. A major influence on many of the Northern School was **Louis MacNeice**, a contemporary at Oxford University of WH Auden, Cecil Day Lewis and Stephen Spender, the "Thirties Poets".

Northern Irish novelists are headed by **CS Lewis** who was born in Belfast in 1898. Although he spent most of his life in England, he retained a fondness for Ireland – in his early years he was influenced by Irish mythology and literature, particularly the works of WB Yeats. Lewis' most famous works are the series of seven children's fantasy novels, *The Chronicles of Narnia* but he was also known for his popular theology and literary criticism.

Other major Northern Irish novelists include: **Forrest Reid**, said to have been the first Ulster novelist of European stature; **Brian Moore** (whose attitude to the city was ambivalent at best); **Glenn Patterson** and **Bernard MacLaverty**.

Although not an author himself, **Patrick Brontë** deserves a mention as father of the Brontë sisters, Anne, Charlotte and Emily. Born into a rural family from Co Down, he was self-educated and changed his name from Brunty when he went to St John's College, Cambridge before becoming a clergyman.

St John Greer Ervine was a unionist playwright, novelist and biographer, said to have been the founding father of modern Northern Irish drama. His works made a naturalistic portrayal of rural and urban life in the North but he had a vehement anti-southern bias which clouded much of his work.

Brian Friel has had major success as a playwright with works such as *Translations*, *Dancing at Lughnasa* and *Philadelphia, Here I Come!*. He co-founded the Field Day Theatre Company with actor Stephen Rea – its aim is to find a middle ground between Ireland's traditional culture and the more secular culture of the north. Its first production was *Translations* in Derry's Guildhall.

Among Ireland's most famous artists are **Paul Henry** and **Sir John Lavery**. Henry is probably the most influential Irish landscape artist of the 20th century, with his post-impressionist paintings of the rugged landscapes of the west. Lavery, knighted in 1918, was best known for his portraits and his paintings can be found in galleries all around the world. Other Northern Irish artists of note include **Basil Blackshaw**, **Frank McKelvey**, **FE McWilliam**, **Markey Robinson**, **Victor Sloan**, **William Conor** and **John Butler Yeats**, father of WB Yeats and Jack Yeats.

Cuisine

Although not particularly noted for its great cuisine, there is one dish that is considered to be part of Ulster's soul:

The **Ulster Fry** is a great cure for a hangover and is not something for the health-conscious to have on a regular basis. It comprises bacon, sausages, eggs, black pudding, tomatoes, as well as soda farl and potato farl. It's a very simple meal to cook.

- Stage 1: heat up the oven; heat up the oil and fry the bacon and sausages until they are brown; put them in the oven.
- Stage 2: with the fat still in the pan, add the soda farl and potato farl, frying them until crispy (but not burnt); into the oven they go.
- Stage 3: in a separate dish, fry the black pudding and tomato.
- Stage 4: crack your eggs into fat in the bacon/farl pan and cook to preference
- Final stage: set it all out on your plate and enjoy!

The soda farls (or soda bread) and potato farls (or potato bread) are a vital part of the recipe. The word farl comes from the Gaelic *fardel*, meaning four parts Here's how to make your own:

Soda farl – you will need two cups of plain flour, a pinch of salt, a teaspoon of baking soda or bicarbonate of soda and a cup of buttermilk. Heat up a pan to a low heat. Put flour and salt in a bowl and mix in the baking soda. Make a well in the middle of the flour and pour in the buttermilk. Stir it all together quickly into a solid, sticky dough; knead the dough gently on a floured surface. Push the dough into a round circle about 2.5 centimetres thick and cut into quarters with a floured knife. Sprinkle some flour into the pan and cook the farls on each side until golden brown (but not burnt).

Potato farl – you will need four medium-sized potatoes, (or a similar amount of mash), a pinch of salt, a small cup of plain flour and a tablespoon of melted butter. Peel and halve the potatoes, then boil them in salted water. Turn off the heat, drain the water and

The Ulster Fry.

return the pan to the hob. While it dries out, mash the potato until smooth (no lumps!). While it's still warm, stir in the flour, salt and melted butter, and mix lightly until doughy. On a floured surface, knead gently until it sticks together. Roll this out into an approximate 20-centimetre (9-inch) circle and cut into quarters. Sprinkle some flour into the pan and cook both sides until they are evenly browned.

One word of advice – if you can get them, use **Comber potatoes**, the best of the spuds in the north.

A good reason for needing a big Ulster Fry is an overindulgence in one of Northern Ireland's favourite products: **Bushmills Whiskey**. The distillery at Bushmills, near the Giant's Causeway, is a popular tourist destination. In 2008, Bushmills celebrated the 400th anniversary of the "license to distil" in Antrim, although the company itself was not founded until 1784.

Sport

Football

George Best
in his prime.

The **Irish Football Association (IFA)**
represents just over 1,500 clubs, and
25,000 registered players. It was founded
in the Queen's Hotel, Belfast, on 18
November 1880 and is the fourth oldest
football association behind its English,
Scottish and Welsh counterparts (the
"home nations"). The IFA is a member
of the International Football Board,
the international rule-making body
comprising four FIFA members and
the four "home nations". Before 1921,
a single side represented all of Ireland;
since then, the IFA has represented
Northern Ireland and the Football
Association of Ireland (FAI) represents
the Republic of Ireland team.

Two innovations that are now
commonplace in world football have
Northern Irish roots:
• William McCrum, the goalkeeper for
Armagh-based club Milford FC came
up with the idea of a penalty kick for
foul play. The proposal was originally
rejected on the grounds that players
were unlikely to kick one another
deliberately but realism prevailed and
the new law was passed in 1891.
• The modern offside law was
introduced in 1925 as a result of the
effective offside tactics employed under
the old rules by Billy McCracken, an
international star of the day who played
for Newcastle United.

The Northern Ireland team has
qualified for three World Cup finals:
they reached the quarter-finals in
Sweden in 1958 and Spain in 1982 and
appeared in the 1986 finals in Mexico.
The team has never qualified for the
European Championship.

Ireland's first international match
was a friendly against England in 1881,
which they lost 13-0 (their record
defeat). They then played in the British
Home Championship, finally winning
the British Championship outright
in 1914, although they then had to
wait until 1980 before winning it
outright again, and in 1984 they won

the last ever British Championship. Northern Ireland's first game against a side outside the Home Nations was their 173rd, against France in Belfast, drawing 2-2. They played France in Paris in 1952 and it wasn't until January 1957 that they met another non home nation team, Portugal, in a World Cup qualifier in Lisbon.

Northern Ireland's biggest win was 7-0 over Wales in 1930. Their biggest victories against non home nations were 5-0 against Albania in 1971 and the Faroe Islands in 1991.

Football Icons

The most famous of all of Northern
Ireland's footballing sons is **George
Best**, known as "the fifth Beatle" and
often said to be the best player never to
play in the World Cup finals – despite
this, Pelé named him as his favourite
player. Born on 22 May 1946, he scored
115 goals in 290 games for Manchester
United, winning two English League
titles in 1965 and 1967. 1968 was his
golden year, winning the European
Cup with United and being voted
European Player of the Year and
Football Writers' Player of the Year.
His powers started to wane through
living the high-life (he said he "got
bored") and he left United at the
end of the 1970 season, aged only 25.

He played for 10 other clubs across the UK, Ireland, USA and Australia. In his international career, he scored nine goals in 37 matches. Despite a liver transplant in 2002, George Best died in November 2005 of multiple organ failure caused by excessive drinking. In 2006, Belfast City Airport was renamed George Best Belfast City Airport in his honour.

The player with most international caps is goalkeeping legend **"Big Pat" Jennings**, with 119 caps; he made his debut in the same game as George Best. Born on 12 June 1945, he spent 13 years at Tottenham Hotspur before making the rare and controversial move to their biggest rivals, Arsenal, where he spent eight years. He played 1,099 games – his only goal came from his own penalty area in the 1967 Charity Shield. He was PFA Player of the Year in 1976 and Football Writers' Player of the Year in 1973. His two most famous international performances came in a 1-0 victory against the 1982 World Cup finals hosts, Spain, and a 0-0 draw against England in 1985, earning the point to carry Northern Ireland to the 1986 World Cup finals.

Danny Blanchflower was born in Belfast on 10 February 1926. The highlight of his playing career was when he captained Tottenham Hotspur to the English League and FA Cup double in 1960-61, aged 34; he won the FA Cup again in 1962 and the European Cup Winners' Cup in 1963; he also played in the 1958 World Cup finals in Sweden. He was the Football Writers' Association Footballer of the Year in 1958 and 1961. He was capped 56 times for Northern Ireland and scored two goals. He was a canny player with natural passing ability and tactical astuteness, a magnetic personality and forthright character.

Others on the Northern Ireland players and managers roll of honour are: **Gerry Armstrong**, 63 caps, 12 goals, 1977-86; **Billy Bingham**, 56 caps, 10 goals, 1951-63 (118 games as manager from 1967-71 and 1980-93; **Mal Donaghy**, 91 caps, no goals, 1980-94; **David Healy**, 74 caps, 35 goals, 2000-present, **Sammy McIlroy**, 88 caps, 5 goals, 1972-87 (manager for 29 games from 2000-03); **Terry Neill**, 59 caps, 2 goals (manager for 20 games from 1971-74); **Martin O'Neill**, 64 caps, 8 goals, 1971-84; **Pat Rice**, 49 caps, no goals, 1968-79; and **Norman Whiteside**, 38 caps, 9 goals, 1982-89.

▲ The GAA Logo.

Gaelic Games

Gaelic football and hurling are run across Ireland by the Gaelic Athletic Association, known commonly by its initials, GAA (in Irish the GAA translates as *Cumann Lúthchleas Gael*). The Ulster provincial council is responsible for organising games within the nine counties of Ulster, including the six counties in Northern Ireland.

Although historically tied in to Irish nationalism – the GAA was banned by the British for a period in 1918 – it has become a much more open organisation and has relaxed many of its protectionist rules, such as bans on members playing other sports (abolished in 1971), the ban on British security forces playing (abolished 2001) and the ban on other sports in GAA grounds (relaxed in 2005 to allow rugby union to be played at its headquarters, Croke Park, while the national rugby stadium was rebuilt).

Northern Irish senior hurling has been the poor cousin to Gaelic football. Antrim are the only county to have made the senior hurling, losing to Cork in 1943, and to Tipperary in 1989.

Northern Irish counties have had more success in senior football, culminating in the 2003 final between two Ulster counties, Tyrone and Armagh. The role of honour reads:

- **Antrim** – runners up twice, in 1911 and 1912.
- **Armagh** – winners in 2002.
- **Derry** – winners in 1993.
- **Down** – five titles: 1960, 1961, 1968, 1991 and 1994.
- **Fermanagh** – runners up in 2008.
- **Tyrone** – three titles: 2003, 2005, 2008.

Gaelic Football Icons

The first recipient of the Texaco Footballer of the Year Award in 1958, **Jim McKeever** (Derry) never won an All Ireland championship but was captain of the Derry team that appeared in that year's final, losing to Dublin.

An All Star in 1971 and 1972, **Sean O'Neill** (Down) is the north's only representative on the GAA's football team of the millennium. He scored 85 goals and more than 500 points for Down's senior team, winning the All Ireland title in 1960, 1961 and 1968.

Other notable names include: **James McCartan**, Down; **Mickey Linden**, Down; **Tony Scullion**, Derry; **Anthony Tohill**, Derry; **Sean Cavanagh**, Tyrone; and **Peter Canavan**, Tyrone.

▲ The Ulster team celebrating after beating Colomiers in rugby union's European Cup final.

Rugby Union

Rugby Union in Ireland, unlike in football/soccer, is run by one body for both Northern Ireland and the Republic of Ireland, the **Irish Rugby Football Union (IRFU)**, established in 1879. The Ulster branch covers the six counties of Northern Ireland plus the three counties in the Republic. The branch has six representatives on the IRFU.

There are currently 56 clubs affiliated to the Ulster branch, with 107 rugby-playing schools (205 and 245

respectively for the IRFU as a whole). The branch regulates the affairs of its clubs and schools and organises inter-provincial matches, club competitions and club matches.

Ulster Rugby represents the whole province in the inter-provincial matches, the Heineken Cup – played against the top teams in European rugby – and the Magners League, played against the top teams from Ireland, Scotland and Wales. The team is based at Ravenhill in Belfast. Rugby is the only sport running a full-time professional team based in Northern Ireland with a full game development structure behind it.

In the era of amateur rugby, Ulster was arguably the most consistently successful of the four provinces (the others being Munster, Leinster and Connacht), and have won the inter-provincial championship 26 times.

The club's greatest achievement came in January 1999, when Ulster won the European Cup, the first Irish province to do so. The team had just eight players playing professional rugby full time – the rest were part-time professionals, having another regular job. It was only later that the club had a roster of only full-time players.

Rugby Icons

Jack Kyle, an outstanding outside-half, won 46 caps for Ireland, scoring seven tries. He was captain and "inspirational genius" of Ireland's Grand Slam-winning team in 1948. His team came close to another Slam three years later when unbeaten but only managing a draw in their final game against Wales. His notoriety as the only Grand Slam-winning Ireland captain ended when he was in Cardiff to watch the 2009 team win its final game. He played six tests for the British and Irish Lions in 1950, against the All Blacks and Australia; his performances in New Zealand were so mesmerising that he is still revered there to this day. In 2002, he was named by the IRFU as the greatest ever Irish rugby player.

A colossus of Irish rugby, in both the literal and metaphorical sense, was **Willie John McBride**. A second row forward for Ballymena, he played a then record 63 caps for Ireland from 1962 to 1975, 11 as captain. In 1973 he set the world record for most consecutive international appearances: 43. He only scored one try for Ireland, in his final game against France, a score that was greeted with a Lansdowne roar as if Ireland had won the Grand Slam itself. His British and Irish Lions record shows he played on five tours, was capped 17 times, and captained them four times. He was captain during the controversial and very physical 1974 Lions tour of South Africa where his imposing presence on the field and charming manner off it helped the "Invincibles" to win the test series 3-0 with one draw. He managed the British Lions in New Zealand in 1983 (a 4-0 loss), the Irish national rugby team (1983-84) and also served on the Irish selection committee (1984-86).

Belfast-born **Mike Gibson** had a highly distinguished career as a centre, out-half and wing for Ireland and the Lions. He broke Willie John's international caps record, winning the final of his 69 Irish caps against Australia in 1979 at the age of 36 – his record lasted 26 years. He toured five times with the Lions, playing in 12 tests, making 66 appearances. Perhaps his greatest hour came in 1971 when the Lions beat New Zealand's All Blacks 2-1, with one draw.

Ballymena and Ireland prop **Syd**

◀ The outstanding forward Willie John McBride.

he coached the Ireland team to their first championship since 1951, was an international selector and was president of the IRFU in 1995-96. He was also chairman of the International Rugby Board and Rugby World Cup Ltd, helping to make the 2007 World Cup in France a commercial success. He was awarded the CBE in 2005 and the *Legion d'honneur* in France in 2007.

Willie Anderson won 27 caps for Ireland between 1984 and 1990. In 1978, on tour with the Penguins rugby club, he was arrested for stealing the Argentine flag from outside a government building and demeaning a patriotic symbol. He spent three months in jail before finally being cleared. His other famous moment came when he stood toe-to-toe with the All Blacks during their traditional *haka* before the game against Ireland in 1989.

Paddy Mayne played for Ireland (six caps) and the Lions (three caps in South Africa, 1938) before his career was cut short by the Second World War. He was also a much-decorated soldier – nominated for a Victoria Cross but getting a fourth DSO (Distinguished Service Order) instead because of his fiery reputation.

Millar won 37 Ireland caps between 1958 and 1970 but his greatest achievements came with the Lions over six decades. He played nine tests in three tours, making 39 Lions appearances in all between 1959 and 1968. Off the pitch, he was an even greater success and has had a major influence on world rugby: he coached the Invincibles in South Africa in 1974, was a selector for the 1977 tour of New Zealand, managed them in the 1980 tour of South Africa and was chairman for the 2001 tour of Australia. In 1974,

Olympics

Northern Ireland's most famous Olympian is undoubtedly **Dame Mary Peters** who won gold in the pentathlon at the 1972 Olympics in Munich. Although born in Halewood, Lancashire, she moved to Ballymena at the age of 11 and considers herself a true Ulsterwoman. She already had two Commonwealth golds in the pentathlon and one in the shot; she had competed at the previous two Olympics, coming fourth in 1964 in Tokyo and ninth at altitude in Mexico. At the age of 33, few expected her to win in Munich against the great Olympian and home favourite, Heidi Rosendahl, who had already won gold in the long jump. The competition came down to the final element, the 200-metre race. Rosendahl won the race with a personal best but Peters came in fourth with yet another personal best

▲ Robin Dixon in the rear of the winning bobsleigh at the 1964 Winter Olympics.

▲ Dame Mary Peters celebrates after receiving the Olympic gold medal for the pentathlon.

Thelma Hopkins was an outstanding Irish athlete, winning silver in the high jump at the Melbourne Olympics in 1956 and competing in the long jump at the same games. She had taken part in both disciplines at the Helsinki games in 1952. In 1956, she also held the high jump world record. Her athleticism was transferred onto the hockey pitch where she won 41 caps for Ireland.

Despite only taking up cycling at the age of 27, **Wendy Houvenaghel** from Co Londonderry won silver for Great Britain and Northern Ireland in the women's 3000-metre cycling pursuit at the Beijing 2008 Olympics. She also won a gold medal in the team pursuit at the 2008 Track World Championships.

The 1964 Winter Olympics in Innsbruck saw **Robin Dixon** win a gold medal in the two-man bobsleigh. Dixon was brakeman to Tony Nash. The gold came partly as a result of the outstanding sportsmanship of one of their Italian rivals, Eugenio Monti, who lent them a spare bolt – needed to keep their bob running after the first run. They followed up their success with gold at the 1965 World Championships, to add to bronze won in 1963 and 1966.

and it was enough for her to win gold with an Olympic and world record 4801 points, 10 points ahead of Rosendahl. Mary Peters' performance came at a time of deep troubles and was a morale-boost across the sectarian divide. She has continued to work tirelessly for athletics in Northern Ireland, many charities and the Northern Ireland Tourist Board and was made a Dame in 2000.

THE LITTLE BOOK OF NORTHERN IRELAND

Boxing

Boxing is a very popular sport in the North and is also run on an all-Ireland basis by the Irish Amateur Boxing Association (IABA). Most boxers elect to box for Ireland at the Olympics but they also qualify for the Great Britain team.

Arguably Ireland's most popular boxer, **Barry McGuigan,** the "Clones Cyclone", was born over the border in Monaghan but was a non-sectarian Ulsterman who was celebrated throughout Ireland. He preferred not to use national symbols, whether the Union Jack or the Tricolour, but used a blue flag with a white dove of peace. He took UK nationality, enabling him to fight for British titles. At the age of 17 he won the featherweight gold at the Commonwealth Games in Edmonton, Canada, in 1978. Turning professional in 1981, he had his first title fight in June 1985 against Eusebio Pedroza at Loftus Road football ground in London in front of 26,000 adoring fans, with a TV audience of more than 20 million. He also went on to be named BBC's Sports Personality of the Year in 1985. He defended his boxing title twice

◀ Barry McGuigan in training.

100 knockouts. He won a gold medal in the 1990 Commonwealth Games and silver at the 1992 Olympic Games in Barcelona. His professional record reads won 27 (18 knockouts), lost seven (two knockouts) but that doesn't tell the full story. Two and a half years after turning professional, he became WBC Bantamweight champion in 1995 and successfully defended his title twice before moving up to Super Bantamweight. He fought for the world titles six times: at Super Bantamweight against Daniel Zaragoza (1997), Erik Morales (1999) and Oscar Larios (2001 twice) and at Featherweight against Prince Naseem Hamed (1998) and Scott Harrison (2004) – he certainly lived up to his reputation as the "best chin in boxing".

Dave "Boy" McAuley was a hard-hitting and determined boxer from Larne who was overshadowed during his flyweight career by Barry McGuigan and never received the recognition he should have. Standing tall for a flyweight at 5' 7", McAuley only had 23 professional fights but nine of these were for versions of the world flyweight title (WBA and IBF versions). He had two epic fights against Colombian boxer

before losing it in June 1986 to the unheralded Steve Cruz in Las Vegas, where he was hospitalised as a result of extreme dehydration. He retired for two years before returning to the ring for four further fights, finally retiring in 1989.

Another of Ireland's top boxers is **Wayne "Pocket Rocket" McCullough** from Belfast. He fought more than 50 international tournaments for Ireland, fighting 319 times and losing only 11 bouts and with over

Other notable Northern Irish boxing personalities include: **Paddy Barnes**; **John Caldwell**; **Freddie Gilroy**; **Rinty Monaghan**; and **Barney Eastwood**.

Motorsports

One of Northern Ireland's greatest sporting icons is **William Joseph "Joey" Dunlop**, a world champion motorcyclist from Ballymoney. In 2005, he was voted as the fifth greatest motorcycling icon ever by *Motorcycle News*. He won 26 Isle of Man TT titles – the only man to win a hat-trick of titles (three in a row) – and five World Championships (in addition to 24 Ulster Grand Prix) and was at home on any type or size of motorbike. He was superstitious, always wearing a yellow helmet, a red t-shirt and riding a number 3 bike. Dunlop was also known for his charitable work with deprived children in Romania and Albania, resulting in him getting an OBE (in addition to his MBE for motorcycling). Dunlop was killed in a motorcycle race in Estonia in 2000 at the age of 48.

Eddie Irvine is a former Formula 1 driver from Newtownards with a Grand

◄◄ Barry McGuigan in action against Eusebio Pedroza.

◄ Joey Dunlop on his way to victory at the TT.

Fidel Bassa which were voted as Fight of the Year in 1986 and 1987. In the first of the two bouts, he came very close to winning when he twice knocked down the undefeated champion in the ninth round before being stopped in the 13th. He won his first IBF title against Duke McKenzie, successfully defending it five times before losing it to Rodolfo Blanco in 1992. His overall record was 8 wins (eight with knockouts), three lost and two drawn.

Prix record of 147 starts, four wins and 26 podium finishes, winning 191 career points. He started his career with Formula Ford, moving through Formula 3 and Formula 3000. He debuted in F1 with panache at the 1993 Japanese Grand Prix with Jordan, finishing in the points after a battle with Ayrton Senna whom he managed to "unlap", having been lapped by the champion; after the race, Senna sought out Irvine in his motorhome and punched him in the face. In 1996 he moved to partner Michael Schumacher at Ferrari, with his best season in 1999 when he won four Grand Prix – Australia, Austria, Germany and Malaysia – finishing second in the drivers' championship, two points behind Mika Hakkinen. After a three-year tenure at Jaguar, he retired from F1 racing in 2002.

Eddie Jordan is best known as the owner of the Formula 1 team, Jordan Grand Prix. With a background as a racer himself at various levels, he then set up his own team in 1980. He formed his F1 team in 1991 and gave Michael Schumacher his debut but was unable to hang on to him. By 1998 he had landed a big enough sponsorship to hire ex-world champion Damon Hill, who won Jordan's first F1 race in a 1-2 with Ralf Schumacher. Despite years of relative success but without an overall championship win, Jordan was unable to sustain the sponsorship levels needed for the sport and had to sell the team in 2004, with the Jordan team's last race in 2005.

Hockey

The **Irish Hockey Association** is the national governing body for field hockey in the whole of Ireland, formed in 2000 after the merger between the two existing unions which governed men's and women's hockey separately.

Stephen Martin from Bangor played in the Great Britain team that won an Olympic gold in Seoul in 1988, the team that won bronze in Los Angeles in 1984 and was captain at the 1992 Barcelona Games. In 2006 he became first chief executive of the Olympic Council of Ireland.

James Kirkwood from Lisburn was a squad member for the team that won gold in Seoul while **Steven Johnston,** who won 20 caps for Ireland mainly at full-back, is best remembered for winning an Olympic bronze with Great Britain at the 1956 Melbourne Games.

Terry Gregg, **Ian Raphael** and **Stewart McNulty** are also IHA Hall of Fame members, with **Sheila Willis** and **Thelma Hopkins** representing the women's game in the Hall of Fame.

Snooker

Northern Irish snooker has produced two world champions: **Alex "Hurricane" Higgins** and **Dennis Taylor**. Higgins won in 1972 and 1982, with runner-up spots in 1976 and 1980. His nickname came from his flamboyant style and the speed

won the Northern Irish Professional Championship every year but one from 1947 to 1972. He was also one of the first players on *Pot Black*, the BBC snooker programme that ran from 1969.

with which he would play. He was also a controversial character, headbutting a tournament director in 1986, and threatening to have his team-mate Dennis Taylor shot at the 1990 World Cup, as well as abusing a referee.

Taylor – noted for his upside-down glasses – was runner-up in 1979 before winning his title in one of Irish sport's, and snooker's, most exciting moments, on the final black ball in the final frame against Steve Davis in 1985, at the age of 36.

A well-known figure in Northern Irish snooker is **Jackie Rea**, who

Golf

With its natural beauty, Northern Ireland is a perfect place to play golf and has a number of outstanding courses, particularly at Royal Portrush and Royal County Down. The country has produced its fair share of great golfers.

Winning The Open at Royal Liverpool in 1947, **Fred Daly** was the only Irishman to have won that title until Padraig Harrington's victory in 2007. He won the title at the age of 36 by one stroke with a score of five over par. He also won the British Matchplay title three times, the Irish Open twice and played in four Ryder Cups.

Darren Clarke, recognisable for smoking large cigars, has won two World Golf Championship titles (2000, 2003) and has finished runner-up in the European Order of Merit on three occasions, in 1998, 2000 and 2003.

In 1997, he finished runner-up in The Open. He has played in five Ryder Cups, most famously in 2006 shortly after the tragic death of his wife, when he won all three of his matches.

Ronan Rafferty won the European Order of Merit in 1989 and was a

Ryder Cup winner in the same year.
He won the Alfred Dunhill Cup for
Ireland in 1988 and 1990.

One of the world's finest young
players is **Rory McIlroy**, who made
his first appearance on the European

Tour in 2005 just a few days after turning 16. In 2009, he finished tied for third in the PGA Championship. He has been picked out by many commentators as a future star, possibly in the Tiger Woods mould.

Other Sporting Icons

Dawson Stelfox, elite adventurer. In May 1993, he became the first Irishman to reach the summit of Mount Everest, leading the expedition up the northeast ridge.

Jim Baker, bowls champion. In 1984, he was World Indoor Singles champion, as well as winning the men's triples titles, he also won the men's fours championship in 1988 and 2004.

Tony "AP" McCoy, national hunt jockey. A man obsessed with his sport, since turning professional in 1995, he has won more than 3,000 races; he has been champion jockey since 1995-96 (to 2008-09). In 2001-02, he rode 289 winners, beating a record which had stood for 55 years. As of 2009, his only serious career failure is not to have won the Grand National.

Richard Dunwoody, national hunt jockey. Dunwoody has won the jockeys' championship three times and has ridden 1,699 winners, second only to AP McCoy. He has won the Grand National twice and the King George VI Chase four times, twice with the legendary grey Desert Orchid. Since retirement, his greatest achievement is reaching the South Pole in 2008 on a charity trek

Eric Smiley, show jumping. Smiley has two bronze medals with Ireland at European Championship level, has represented Ireland at three World Equestrian Games and has been on four Olympic teams.

Irish cricket team, 1969. One of the greatest cricket upsets of all time took place in Belfast when Ireland's amateurs skittled out a West Indies team led by the great Clive Lloyd for 25 runs, and won by nine wickets. Rumour has it that the large rounds of Guinness offered by the hosts the night before may have had something to do with the result. Ireland is now an established cricket team, taking part regularly in the ICC trophy, in the World Cup 2007, famously beating Pakistan, and in the 2009 World Twenty20.

◀ Richard Dunwoody winning the 1994 Grand National.

National Identity

Flags and Symbols

The Union Jack flying outside Belfast City Hall

The Ulster flag being hung up prior to a football match.

Province of Ulster flag

This represents the nine counties of Ulster, one of the four provincial flags of Ireland.

Government of Ulster flag

Also known as the Ulster flag. Much used by unionists and is based on the St George's cross, with the Crown, Star of David and the Red Hand of Ulster.

St Patrick's Cross

This is not much used in the general population and is seen as a British symbol, used by army regiments.

Union Jack
This is the official flag of Northern Ireland, used by unionists to demonstrate their loyalty to the United Kingdom of Great Britain and Northern Ireland.

Irish National flag (Tricolour)
Ireland's national flag is designed to signify the peace (white) between nationalists (green) and unionists (orange).

Orange Order flag
An orange flag with a purple star, the symbol of Williamite forces.

Crimson flag
The Apprentice Boys' flag, symbolising their bloody resistance at the Siege of Londonderry.

Red Hand
Used by the Protestant community to

▲ The Irish National flag (Tricolour).

▶ A shamrock.

▶▶ A mural on a wall in East Belfast.

signify the six counties, it is found on the Ulster provincial flag, representing all nine counties. It is believed to originate from a mythical tale where two chieftains were racing across a stretch of water to reach and claim land. Realising his enemy would get there first, one of them cut off his hand and threw it onto shore, claiming the land.

Celtic harp

Also known as Brian Ború's harp. On its own, it represents the Irish tradition but it

is used by unionists with a crown on it, for example as used by the RUC on their caps.

Flax flower

The flax flower is used as a symbol of peace in Northern Ireland and is the emblem of the Assembly.

Shamrock

The three-leafed clover is a symbol of Ireland, north and south, particularly with reference to St Patrick who is believed to have used it to demonstrate the Holy Trinity. It is worn on 17 March, St Patrick's Day.

▶ Belfast mural.

Murals

Murals are used by both nationalists and unionists to commemorate events and battles. They appear particularly in working class areas of Northern Ireland. Sash, bowler hat and white glovesPart of the traditional clothing worn by members of the Orange Order. White/green/orange ribbons White represents peace, green is used by nationalists and orange by unionists.

Sash, bowler hat and white gloves

Part of the traditional clothing worn by members of the Orange Order.

White/green/orange ribbons

White represents peace, green is used by nationalists and orange by unionists.

Anthems

A number of songs are used prominently in the north, often by both communities.

A Londonderry Air: since its "discovery" in the mid-19th century, the tune has had various lyrics down the years but the most well known is *Danny Boy*, written by Frederick Weatherly in 1913: "Oh Danny Boy, the pipes, the pipes are calling/From glen to glen, and down the mountain side…"

Ireland's Call: the anthem for the rugby team of Ireland: "Come the day/ And come the hour/Come the power and the glory/We have come to answer/ Our country's call…/From the four proud provinces of Ireland…"

The Sash: a unionist ballad commemorating King William's victory in the war against the Jacobites: "Sure I'm an Irish Orangeman, from Erin's isle I came/To see my foreign brethren all of honour and of fame/And to tell them of my forefathers who fought in days of yore/That I might have the right to wear the sash my father wore!"

The Town I Loved So Well: written by Phil Coulter about his home town of Derry.

The Mountains of Mourne: written by Percy French abwout the Irish diaspora wishing to return home.

Languages

There are three officially recognised languages in Northern Ireland. The main language is English, spoken by the whole population.

Can It Change?

Belfast Telegraph

Several hundred familys were forced to flee their homes last night as houses came under attack from republicans. The number of homeless is running into several thousand, more people were moving out of riot areas today. The women and children have been offered shelter in cities across the sea. Security forces moved in to bring calm into riot areas.

Belfast Telegraph

?

We believe!

Irish, or Gaelic, is spoken by approximately 5% of the population. The Irish Language Agency (*Foras na Gaeilge*) was set up after the Good Friday Agreement to promote the language.

Ulster Scots (*Ullans*) is a recognised regional language and the Ulster–Scots Agency (*Tha Boord o Ulstèr-Scotch*) has been set up to promote the language and culture of the Ulster Scots. There are approximately 35,000 speakers.

▶ Belfast at night.

THE LITTLE BOOK OF NORTHERN IRELAND

Other books also available:

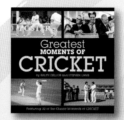
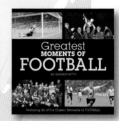

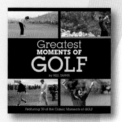

Available from all major stockists

LITTLE BOOK OF THE
OLYMPICS
AN OLYMPIC A to Z
Written by Ian Stroud

THE LITTLE BOOK OF
HORSERACING
A HORSERACING A to Z
Written by Jenny Whitmore and Claire Slattery

The Little Book of
CRICKET
LEGENDS
RALPH DELLOR and STEPHEN LAMB

The Little Book of
GOLF
LEGENDS
Neil TAPPIN

The Little Book of
FOOTBALL
LEGENDS
GRAHAM BETTS

The Little Book of
RUGBY
LEGENDS
PAUL MORGAN and ALEX MEAD

The Little Book of
GRAND PRIX
LEGENDS
PHILIP RABY

THE LITTLE BOOK OF
EUROPEAN FOOTBALL
Written by Graham Betts

THE LITTLE BOOK OF
FISHING
Angler's Mail
A FISHING A to Z
Written by Rob Yorke

THE LITTLE BOOK OF
JANE AUSTEN

LITTLE BOOK OF THE
BRONTË SISTERS

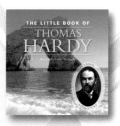
THE LITTLE BOOK OF
THOMAS HARDY

Available from all major stockists

The pictures in this book were provided courtesy of the following:

GETTY IMAGES
101 Bayham Street, London NW1 0AG

SHUTTERSTOCK
www.shutterstock.com

Creative Director: Kevin Gardner

Design and Artwork: David Wildish

Picture research: Ellie Charleston

Published by Green Umbrella Publishing

Publishers Jules Gammond and Vanessa Gardner

Written by Mike Henigan